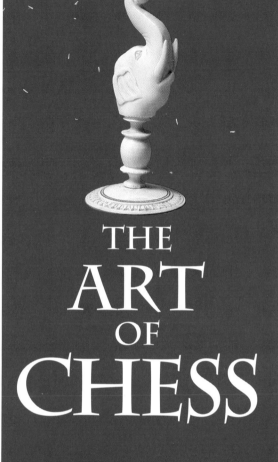

THE
ART
OF
CHESS

Harry N. Abrams, Inc., Publishers

COLLEEN
SCHAFROTH

THE
ART
OF
CHESS

To my husband and daughter, Stephen and Elizabeth Schafroth, who not only supported me, but continued to love me throughout this time-consuming project.

Produced by
Richard J. Berenson
Berenson Design & Books, Ltd., New York

Library of Congress Cataloging-in-Publication Data

Schafroth, Colleen.
    The art of chess / Colleen Schafroth.— 1st ed.
        p. cm.
    Includes bibliographical references and index.
    ISBN 0–8109–1001–2
     1. Chess—History. I. Title.

GV1317.S32 2002
794.1'09—dc21   2001053618

Printed and bound in Belgium

10 9 8 7 6 5 4 3 2 1

Harry N. Abrams, Inc.
100 Fifth Avenue
New York, N.Y. 10011
www.abramsbooks.com

Abrams is a subsidiary of

On page 1:
Bishop, India, Sahib style,
ivory, 19th century

On pages 2 and 3:
Left to right: Chess set, Italy, stone, 1957;
Faience set and board, French,
Régence style, ceramic, 19th–20th century;
Queen, Barleycorn style, Great Britain,
bone, 19th century;
"The Three Sisters Playing Chess," 1555,
by Sofonisba Anguissola (1527–1625);
African king, French, Dieppe style,
ivory, c. 1750.

CONTENTS

INTRODUCTION

THE GAME OF CHESS is unlike any other game. It has been played from time immemorial across landscapes and cultures both foreign and exotic to modern eyes. Its legends and stories tell of rising and falling nations, battles and intrigue, heroes and lovers, cowards and thieves. Of all the games that have been invented, few if any can claim its allure, drama, mystery, and romance. Even its origin is shrouded in the mists of the distant past; to take hold and understand its ancient history is like grasping wispy tendrils of fog. Seemingly solid, they quickly evaporate into the night air.

The history of chess is a story of transformation. As various societies took possession of the game, they altered it according to their own interests and needs. Rules were bent or completely changed before it was passed on to another group of people. Numerous variants flared up, to fade away while others thrived and still exist in one part of the world or another. Over the centuries, chess gradually transformed from an ancient game of war into one of intellectual pursuit. It became civilized.

In many ways, it is the playing pieces themselves that tell us the

KING, INDIAN, IVORY, C. 1930S

This king represents Ravana, the ten-headed demon king who opposes the hero, Rama, in the ancient Hindu epic, the *Ramayana*. The epic tells the story of Prince Rama and his exploits. As the story progresses, Rama marries a beautiful woman named Sita. Due to political intrigue, Rama is unjustly banished from court and retreats to a forest where the demon king, Ravana, seizes Sita and carries her off. The rest of the epic describes Rama's attempt to gain her release. This ancient Hindu epic inspired carvers throughout southern Asia.

INTRODUCTION

story of chess. Outwardly they imply the hostilities of battle, one side against the other. But they are much more than that. Chess sets are cultural icons reflecting layers of meaning both deliberately and unintentionally imposed on the pieces by the individuals who made them—people working under the influence of their society, time, and place. Thus, the pieces have become tangible, evocative remains of the past. As chess moved from culture to culture, the pieces were molded into new shapes and images reflecting fresh surroundings.

At the same time, the names of the pieces were translated into other languages and sometimes given new meanings. Chess pieces have frequently taken on political, cultural, or artistic significance beyond their practical value. Look behind the superficial appearance of individual pieces. Chess sets are like mirrors reflecting human history and culture.

On the more pragmatic side are the artistic problems and solutions related to the design of a superior chess set. The maker must answer many questions and choose from seemingly endless options when creating thirty-two pieces based on a central theme intended to stimulate

KING, BALI, STAGHORN, 20TH CENTURY

Figural chess sets, like this one, were carved for the tourist trade. Bali carvers were often inspired by Hindu stories.

ITALY, CARVED, GILDED AND PAINTED WOOD, C. 1960S

The carver of this set may have based the design on figural chess sets of the Renaissance. The board is composed of four separate sections, each containing a drawer in which the pieces reside. The theme of the set portrays the Italians against the Saracens—alluding perhaps to a time when the Arabs dominated parts of southern Italy. It was Arab chess enthusiasts who perhaps first introduced the game to the Italians sometime in the 10th century.

8

interest, and even excitement. Is the set's purpose simply functional, ornamental, or some combination of the two? Should the images be representational, symbolic, or abstract? What are the available materials: ivory, wood, bone, glass, precious metal, or plastic? Should the set be hand-carved, lathed, molded, or assembled?

Indeed, the game of chess has occupied the time and stirred the passions of untold generations. People from all walks of life, from royal courts to inner cities, have been drawn to it—playing the game, making the sets, studying the theories and the history, speculating on the future, and even helping to shape that future by creating new variations. Hold a chess piece in your hand and you grasp a world, representing a myriad of ideas and cultures going back well over a thousand years. Few man-made objects can claim such distinction.

SOVIET RUSSIA, PORCELAIN, 2OTH CENTURY

This set, in which the Soviets are pitted against the Capitalists, makes a unique statement about political ideologies as seen by the Soviets. The Capitalists, represented by pawns bound in chains, a licentious queen and king represented by death, present an unflattering view of the West while the opposing side, represented by farmers, workers, and a youthful, wholesome king and queen, present the Soviets as the moral victors. The set was designed by the sisters Natalia and Yelena Danko and manufactured by the Lomonosov Porcelain Factory over several decades. It was first introduced in 1922.

CHAPTER ONE
ORIGINS OF THE GAME

GAMES OF ALL KINDS have existed for thousands of years. Common to people everywhere, they first appear in the archaeological record just when human societies began to form. The earliest may have been devised for religious purposes or as models to understand the complexities of life in a safe and controlled manner. Whether they were games of chance or strategy, ancient games shared certain similarities. They were easily made, often used small gaming pieces, and were played on boards of some kind. Over time, a number of enduring games emerged and evolved out of this primeval group. Chess was one of them.

When and where chess originated has been seriously debated for centuries. Scholars of the past, convinced of the game's nobility, have credited its invention to an array of cultures and individuals from antiquity. These include the Greeks, Egyptians, Hebrews, Babylonians, Scythians, Chinese, Indians, Persians, and Arabs. The cast has included Xerxes, Solomon, Aristotle, Hippocrates, any number of rajahs, viziers, sultans, and even Adam.

KING(?),
ARABIC, AFTER
AN INDIAN MODEL,
IVORY,
8TH-10TH CENTURY

Even though this figure may not in fact be a chess piece, its age and style (reminiscent of more recent sets from India) suggests a naturalistic model that the Arabs most likely acquired with the game of chess after their conquest of Persia in 651. Early Arab artisans synthesized its shape and form to create abstracted sets of great economy and beauty. Legend has it that this piece was given to Emperor Charlemagne (742–814) by Harun al Raschid (765–809), Caliph of Baghdad. Inscriptions on its base suggest that it was made near Basra in Iraq.

Historians and scholars of the game have zealously searched ancient texts, especially from China, India, and Persia, for evidence of the origins of chess. Although passing references to a game that is clearly chess can be found in texts from as early as about 600, the oldest surviving books that describe the game in some detail date back only to the ninth century. Even though the earliest of these known historic documents form the basis for much of the speculation about the origins and precursors of chess, it is important to remember that in many cases early accounts were, in fact, retold, copied, or written down centuries later, losing some of their credibility in the process. Nevertheless, despite the difficulty of sorting out fact from fiction, the story of chess is gradually emerging out of the mist and into the light.

PRECURSORS TO THE GAME

A recent reinterpretation of ancient Chinese texts has encouraged some scholars to suggest that chess may have originated as a Chinese game of divination—interpretation of signs to foretell the future—during the reign of Wu Ti (560–578), an emperor of the short-lived Northern Chou (now spelled Zhou) dynasty in western China. One Chinese text, *T'ai ping yu lan*, revised in 984, suggests that that emperor discovered *hsiang ch'i* (now *xiang qi*), the Chinese term for chess, and describes the pieces and their moves as having been designed after the sun, moon, planets, and "star-houses" (constellations). Later it was recorded that T'ai Tsung (reigned 626–649),

ROOK, (CHARLEMAGNE CHESSMAN), ITALY, IVORY, 11TH CENTURY

At the time the Arabs acquired the game of chess, sometime in the 7th–8th centuries, the chariot had long been associated with the rook. This has led some scholars to suggest an earlier date for the invention of chess than literary, historical and archaeological sources might warrant. Since the use of the chariot as a military weapon was largely discontinued throughout the ancient world after the 4th century, they suggest that chess must have been invented when chariots were commonplace, and a likely candidate for representing a chess piece. This rook, one of sixteen surviving chess pieces, was probably carved in southern Italy. At the time, Italy was a melting pot of cultures. The Byzantine Emperor laid claim to much of the Italian Peninsula while the Arabs controlled Sicily and parts of the Peninsula. At the same time, the Normans from northern Europe were trying to wrest control of the region from both.

the second emperor of the T'ang (Tang) dynasty, also played a game called chess, perhaps derived from Wu Ti's divination game. The nagging conundrum is that the Chinese term for chess may actually refer to no less than three types of games played during the reign of T'ai Tsung. If the divinatory game of Wu Ti is indeed a prototype, then it may be the ancestor of both Chinese chess played throughout Asia today, and the Western game which subsequently developed in India.

Although a precursor or variant may have existed in China, most historians believe that chess in fact originated in India, perhaps as early as the fifth or sixth century, if not before. Direct evidence is scant, but the claim can be supported. The cornerstone of the argument is the assertion by several early Arabic authorities that India was the birthplace of chess, not Persia, where the Arabs first learned to play the game in the seventh century.

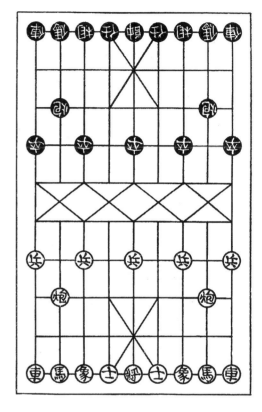

Left:
These men are absorbed in a game of Chinese chess. This game, a cousin of the one played in the West, has existed for centuries. Some historians have suggested that chess originated in China and spread both east and west around the world.

Above:
As the diagram from H.J.R. Murray's *A History of Chess* shows, Chinese chess is played with round flat discs (distinguished by Chinese characters) on the intersecting lines of the squares. The king resides in a fortress comprised of four squares, and the middle of the board is divided by an imaginary river which limits access to the opposing side.

17

One of the earliest documents to suggest that chess traveled into Persia from India is in an early seventh-century Persian collection of stories known as the *Chatrang-namak*. Nearly four centuries later, the famous Persian poet Abul Kasim Mansur, better known by his pen name Firdawsi (c. 940?–1020?), retold the same story in his monumental epic, the *Shah Namah (Book of Kings)*. Firdawsi relates that a rajah of India sent the game of chess—without any explanation of the rules—as a riddle to King Khosrau I (reigned 528–579), also called Anüshirvan, of Persia. Thanks to a minister variously named Bozorgmehr or Wajurgmitr in subsequent texts and translations, the king solves the riddle—thus avoiding payment of tribute—and returns the answer to the rajah along with his own riddle in the form of the game of *nards* (backgammon). In both the *Chatrang-namak* and the *Shah Namah*, chess is described as a game for two opponents played

ILLUMINATION, PERSIA, OPAQUE WATERCOLOR AND INK, TRANSCRIBED 1553

The national Persian epic, the *Shah Namah*, retells the story of Persia from the earliest Persian ruler to the last Sassanid king in 651. Among the stories told, is one about chess. This page illustrates the moment when the Indian legation to the Court of Shah Anüshirvan (528–579) arrives, carrying with them the game of chess as a riddle for the shah. The shah's wiseman solves the puzzle presented, and the shah returns it in triumph to the rajah of India, with their own riddle, *Nards* or backgammon. The *Shah Namah*, penned by the Persian poet Firdawsi (940?–1020?) around 1010, became extremely popular. Over the next several centuries, many transcriptions of the book, often accompanied with exquisite illuminations, were commissioned by various Shahs and Caliphs throughout the Islamic empire.

وزوكردوانديشه باربكر | | بكه كردجاى كه تايك تر
بانديشها نرو راپازكرد | خردبادل روشن انبازكرد | بكه كردبغنو ورنج روان | بشطرنج وانديشه مندوان
دوروبه برآرآراسته كارزار | يكى رزكه بباخت شطرنج وآ | همه يك علاج هرنانس ساج | وهمه بغمودن دل زعلاج

دوشاه بخشيد بهشت خوى | زمين باددشكركه چارسوى | همه رزم جويان كرنده شهر | دوشكربخشيد درهشت بهر
كرازان دوشاه اندران نگار | بهرجاى كرش دكراپرد | يكى زان دكرزكمر دستم | كدرازاندقت رهروبهم

ILLUMINATION,
PERSIAN,
"TREATISE ON THE
GAME OF CHESS,"
OPAQUE WATERCOL-
OR AND INK,
TRANSCRIBED
16TH CENTURY

Over the centuries, Islamic chess scholars and players wrote extensively about the game. They not only delved into the early history of it, but wrote biographical lists of the outstanding players and presented the great chess problems of their day. This manuscript praises Ali Shatranji, the renowned player at the Court of Timur (Tamerlane, 1336–1405) and contains a history of chess, an analysis of playing pieces, several problems, and a description of a chess variant known as *Timur's Great Game*. Although not illustrated here, the latter game, played on a board of 110 squares, has achieved a certain notoriety over time because it was an apparent favorite of the ruler. The author of the work may possibly be Ali Shatranji himself.

on a board of sixty-four squares. The pieces are represented as foot soldiers, elephants, chariots, horses, the counselor, and the king.

Recent archaeological findings support the view that chess was known in Persia before the Arab conquest of the mid-seventh century. In 1977, seven small ivory carvings dated as early as the seventh century were found in the ancient site of Afrasiab in Samarkand, now in Uzbekistan. They have subsequently been interpreted as chess pieces, and they strongly recall the descriptions of Persian sets by writers such as Firdawsi. The figures include a *shah* (king), *farzin* (counselor), *pil* (elephant), *asp* (horse), *rukh* (chariot), and *pujada* (foot soldier).

These pieces, along with the descriptions of the game found in the *Chatrang-namak* and the *Shah Namah*, bear some noteworthy resemblance to a description of chess in a Sanskrit text from the twelfth century, the *Manasollasa*. This work describes chess as a game of skill played by two competitors, and it lists two variants of the game. One of these is *chaturanga* (Sanskrit for "four members").

In this game, four players compete using four different symbolic armies subordinate to a king. These eight-piece armies represent the four main military branches of the ancient world: chariot, elephant, cavalry, and infantry led by the king. Pieces were distributed in the four corners of the sixty-four-square board, dice were sometimes thrown, and play continued until all of a player's opponents were eliminated. Descriptions of this game found in Indian texts have led some scholars to suggest that *chaturanga* is a direct ancestor of chess. Not only do some of the rules, the pieces, and the board suggest a rela-

In 1030 an Arab scholar, Al-Beruni, wrote one of the first descriptions of the Indian game of *chaturanga*. A more complete description is given in the 12th-century Sanskrit manuscript, the *Manasollasa (Joy of the Mind)*. It describes the game as being comprised of four symbolic armies—the chariots, cavalry, elephants, and infantry ruled by a king. As is diagrammed here in H.J.R. Murray's *A History of Chess*, the pieces were lined up on the four corners of the *ashtapadas* (or board). In some descriptions the game is played with dice. In the *Manasollasa*, the dice are not used. Later accounts of the game reflect a Persian-Arab influence, suggesting that if *chaturanga* developed from chess, it did so before the Arabs knew the game.

CHESS SET
MUSLIM (INDIA?)
IVORY
18TH CENTURY

The distinctive spool shapes of this elegant set suggest that it may be of Indian origin. Sets similar to this one have been documented as early as the 17th century. After the conquest of Persia in the 7th century, Arab leaders slowly began to exert their influence west across North Africa, and east into India. Although chess originated in India, the Arabs probably introduced their version of the game to India as they gained control over parts of the country sometime in the 11th century. Undoubtedly, at the same time, they also introduced conventional-style playing pieces, like these, commonly used throughout the Arab world.

tionship between *chaturanga* and chess, but also the nomenclature of the game. The Arabic word for chess, *shatranj,* is derived from the Persian term, *chatrang,* which in turn appears to have come from the Sanskrit *chaturanga.* Despite some significant differences, *chaturanga* is clearly associated with the game of chess. However, since definitive references appear side-by-side with those of chess, other scholars have suggested that *chaturanga* was a variant that evolved after chess was established in India and possibly Persia.

Even if Firdawsi's tale has an element of truth in it, it does not resolve when and where a recognizable game of chess actually appeared. When was the use of dice discarded? When did it become a two-player game? Did chess evolve in Persia after its arrival from India? Indeed, was the Persian *chatrang* influenced by *chaturanga*—or was the Indian game influenced by chess? Is chess perhaps a combination of *chaturanga* and other games played in the region, such as the ancient Greek game of *Petteia*? In the end, there are far more questions about the beginnings of chess than answers. Unfortunately, the true origins of chess are likely to remain murky until more archaeological or historical evidence comes to light.

THE SPREAD OF THE GAME

That a discernible game of chess appeared in Persia and was subsequently appropriated by the Arabs suggests that wherever it originated, the game was known in Persia, and probably in

northern India, by about the fifth or sixth century. A growing number of literary references, as well as the appearance of physical evidence, tells us that by the eighth or ninth century, the game had already begun to spread simultaneously outward, perhaps along the famous trade route known as the Silk Road. The variant known in Asia today as Chinese chess may have come from India before spreading northeastward into Korea and finally, by the eleventh century, to Japan, where it was further adapted. At about the same time, the game also spread from India to the southeastern end of the Asian continent, into Burma, Indochina, and the Malay Peninsula, where the game more closely follows the version played in India. Meanwhile, as a result of Arab invasion and conquest, the Persian game traveled west and south into parts of the African continent, as well as northwest, reaching Europe within two or three centuries. By the beginning of the eleventh century, perhaps five or six hundred years after its establishment, chess was being played throughout much of the known world—a remarkable achievement for a board game.

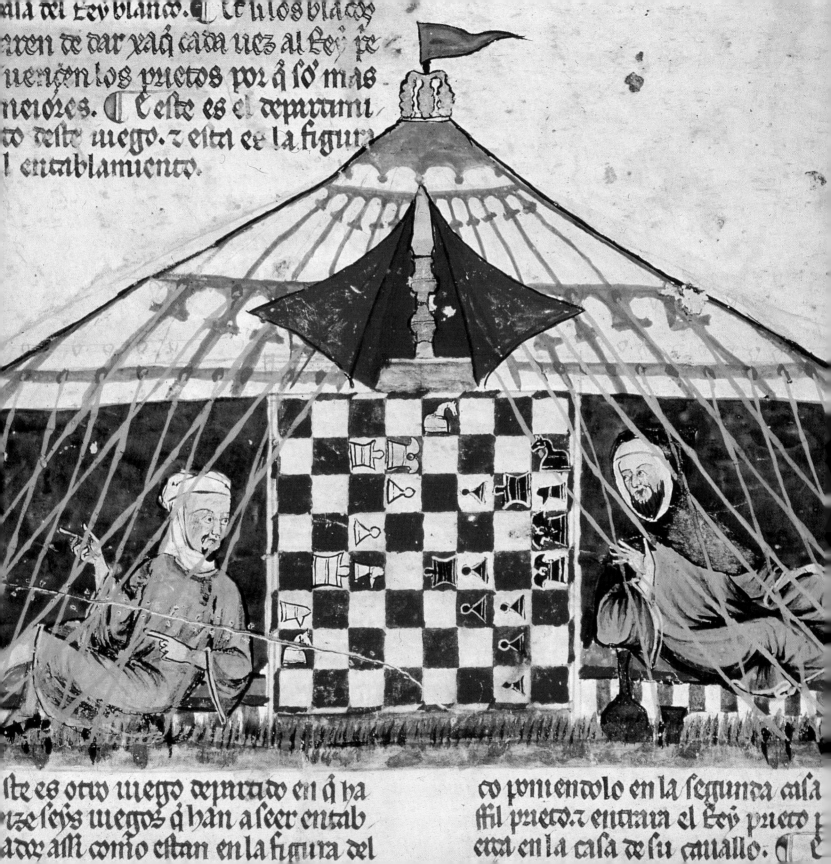

CHAPTER TWO
THE FIRST GOLDEN AGE OF CHESS

THE ARABS ADOPTED CHESS, which they called *shatranj*, sometime after their conquest of Persia in the mid-seventh century. The period that followed was a dynamic one for the burgeoning Arab culture. Chess was only one small facet of the multicultural influences from Persia, Greece, Byzantium, Egypt, and other nearby civilizations that Arab scholars, historians, scientists, mathematicians, and poets assimilated and made their own. And like their other cultural acquisitions, they took the game with them into the far-flung corners of their rapidly growing empire, from India to Spain.

The earliest known clear references to chess in Arabic literature date from the early eighth century. The poet al-Farazdaq wrote, "I keep you from your inheritance and from the royal crown so that, hindered by my arm, you remain a Pawn among the Pawns." Since the word used for pawn, *baidaq*, has no other meaning in Arabic than the chess piece, it is clear that the game not only had been established in the Arab world by the eighth century, but may have

ILLUMINATION, SPAIN, OPAQUE WATERCOLOR AND GOLD LEAF, 1283

Shortly before his death the Spanish King, Alfonso X (reigned 1252–1284), commissioned a book, *Libros del axedrez, dados et tablas,* about the games of chess, dice, and tables (or backgammon). The book includes 103 chess problems as well as several variants of the game, including decimal chess and four-handed chess. Although a small number of the problems presented have a European ancestry, the majority of them derive from earlier Muslim sources. Alfonso the Wise was a poet, scientist, legislator, historian, and patron of education and the arts.

**KNIGHT,
EURO-ARABIC,
IVORY,
8TH-9TH CENTURY**

This knight is typical of
Arabic playing pieces
of the period. The figure
lacks any physical features,
such as eyes and ears,
which would have animated
it, evoking the presence of
the horse behind the piece.
For a couple of centuries
following the introduction
of chess into Europe,
Europeans were content
to use Arabic-style pieces.

been popular enough to be used as common reference in poetry. By the
first decade of the eleventh century, when Firdawsi retells the tale of
how chess came to Persia in his national epic the *Shah Namah*, it is evi-
dent that the game is well established in Arab society.

At least from the ninth and well into the twelfth century, Arab players spent a considerable amount of time and effort focusing on chess,
enriching as well as expanding the game. During this early golden age,
it flourished under the patronage of a number of caliphs throughout
the empire. Indeed, court champions were lionized and their exploits
were compiled in several collections. One such collection, which Ibn
an-Nadim wrote in 988, lists several succeeding generations of players,
including two chess masters, al-Adli and ar-Razi, who lived and com-
peted in the mid-ninth century at the court of Caliph al-Mutawakkil
(reigned 847–861).

A number of these noted players took pen in hand and began to
write some of the first comprehensive descriptions of the game. These
early chess treatises, which included strategies, tactics, and some of the
first recorded chess problems, were commissioned by caliphs and
shahs throughout the region. Many of these works also included chess-
related stories, both true and fantastic. Among the better-known
books were those written by the famous chess master as-Suli, a leading
player during the reign of Caliph al-Muktafi (902–908), and his pupil
al-Lajlaj. Such was their fame that stories and commentaries from their
books on chess survived in collections published well into the thirteenth century, and sporadically much later.

CHESS SET, EURO-ARABIC, BONE, 8TH-9TH CENTURY

Arabic sets, like this one, were based on the severe reduction of earlier Persian representational models down to an abstracted synthesis of form and shape. The sensual line and suppleness of form create a sophistication of design unequaled until the Staunton style was introduced in the 19th century. Other known sets of this type, such as the 10th-century Ubar set found in Oman, or the one discovered in an 11th-century shipwreck off the coast of Turkey, testify to the universality of this style throughout the Islamic world. Although this set may have been manufactured in Europe, it is also possible that it was brought back to Europe during the First Crusade (1095–1099). This style would remain in use until at least the 13th century.

Despite its popularity, there were times when chess risked condemnation by religious leaders. Although it was not specifically proscribed by the Koran (which predated Arab knowledge of the game), many leaders considered chess to be frivolous. A stronger charge against it was that, like other games, it was often associated with gambling—thereby violating Islamic law and precedent. Arab players countered these accusations by justifying the game as an educational tool used solely to train the intellect and instruct leaders about the strategy of warfare. Similar objections and justifications would later be offered by the European clergy on the one hand and fans of the game on the other following its introduction to Europe.

EARLY PLAYING PIECES

Because examples of playing pieces are virtually unknown prior to the Arab conquest of Persia in the seventh century, little is known about their early appearance. Arabic sources describe Persian sets, and by inference Indian ones, as a series of representational pieces portraying real armies. The previously mentioned discovery of several ivory chess pieces in the ruins of Samarkand, dated to the eighth or possibly the seventh century, substantiates early Arabic accounts: the pieces depict the elephants, horses, chariots, rulers, and foot soldiers of the ancient world.

Similar pieces, crafted in the eighth or ninth century and purportedly a gift to Emperor Charlemagne by Caliph Harun al-Rashid (reigned

**BISHOP,
(CHARLEMAGNE
CHESSMAN),
ITALY, IVORY,
LATE 11TH–
EARLY 12TH CENTURY**

This bishop is one of sixteen surviving pieces from a chess set made in southern Italy at the end of the 11th century. At the time it was made, Arabs, Normans, and the Byzantine Empire were battling for control of the Italian Peninsula. The use of the elephant to represent the bishop may suggest an Eastern influence on the maker, perhaps from Constantinople. Arab artists abstracted the shape and form of the Persian elephant playing piece (bishop), like this one, reducing it to a simple shaft with two distinct knobs protruding from the top to represent the elephant's tusks.

786–809), and a late-eleventh-century set from southern Italy both strongly suggest an Eastern influence not only in their representation of elephants and chariots but in the stylistic elements reminiscent of Indian and Persian work. These sets and the descriptions left by early Arabic writers, however, provide a less than comprehensive picture of what representational chess sets might have looked like more than a thousand years ago.

CONVENTIONAL PLAYING PIECES

Whatever the actual form chess pieces took in India and Persia, it is likely that Arab players initially used them as well. It was probably not long, however, before Arab artisans began to adapt the Persian models to their own needs and concerns. Although representational art was not strictly forbidden by the Koran, it was discouraged. Accordingly, the makers of games may have attempted to minimize the uneasiness of religious authorities toward chess by adopting conventional, or abstracted, designs for the playing pieces. Such designs may also have reflected the desire of players to have compact pieces for greater ease of play.

Conventional designs, employing simplified, abstracted, or symbolic shapes and forms, had been used as game markers for centuries before the inven-

30

tion of chess. Game markers and playing pieces dating from the second and third centuries B.C.E. found along the banks of the Indus River, are conventional in form. Even older games, such as the Egyptian board game of *Senet*, commonly used conventional-style playing pieces. In fact, there is no reason to believe that chess pieces of a conventional manner did not already exist side by side with Persian or Indian representational chess figures prior to the Arabs' adoption of the game.

By choosing conventional designs, Arab players may simply have selected the style that suited them best, both philosophically and practically. In time, they became masters of the conventional form, distilling a playing piece to its essence in a reserved but elegant manner. Further, Arab ingenuity created not one but two distinctly different conventional types, providing players with an aesthetic choice.

To some extent, one style was determined by the lathe on which it was made. Originally powered by a foot-operated treadle, a lathe is a turning machine that allows an operator to remove unwanted material from a cylindrical object by rotating it against a cutting tool. Although the origin of the lathe is almost as obscure as chess, it existed widely throughout the ancient world.

Arab chess pieces made on a lathe are generally clean and spare in design. They are conceived as shafts on pedestals. For the most part, the function of each piece is determined by its height and width, which may have originally been based on the height relationships among the pieces in the original Persian or Indian model. The Arab pieces

**BAS RELIEF,
EGYPT,
PAINTED STONE,
19TH DYNASTY**

Games of chance and skill, such as the Egyptian game of *Senet*, have been played for thousands of years. Although chess can only be documented as far back as the 6th century, gaming pieces and boards of all shapes and sizes have been found throughout the ancient world. Certainly, the development of these games set the stage for the invention of chess centuries later.

CHESS SET, PERSIA, PAINTED WOOD, 19TH CENTURY

After their adoption of chess, Arab artisans over time gradually developed two distinct types of chessmen. One was a highly abstracted style based on an earlier Persian representational model. The other, illustrated here, is comprised of nonrepresentational pieces turned on a lathe. Thirty-seven pieces, dating from the 11th century and found at an archaeological site in Bambra-ka-thul, India, were, like these, turned on a lathe. Although not conclusive, these pieces suggest that both styles may share a common history and age. Today, lathe-turned pieces are a favorite type found throughout Islam.

may be plain, stained, or decoratively inscribed with small geometric shapes wrapped around their perimeters. Some of the earliest known chess pieces of this type were found in the ruins of a Muslim city near present-day Hyderabad in Pakistan. They date from the early decades of the eleventh century when the town was destroyed by an earthquake. Conventional designs similar to these are still found today in many Muslim countries.

The other style, a masterpiece of design, was based on a completely abstracted version of the older Persian and Indian representational models (see the illustration on page 27). Usually hand-carved, each playing piece was reduced to its basic elementary form in an economy of design that was both sensuous and sophisticated. Thus, the king and counselor became spare cylindrical shafts with a curve cut into one side to symbolize a figure seated on a throne or in the *howdah* atop an elephant. The elephant was symbolized by a stocky piece, recalling the grandeur and mass of the animal, with two projections suggesting the tusks. The horse more closely resembled its original model, with a severely stylized head and neck. The chariot, formed by the contour line of the horse, chariot, and rider as seen from the side, was perhaps the furthest removed from the representational source. In addition, the piece symbolizing the foot soldier was often expressed by a simple compact shaft. This elegant abstract style would be used at least until the thirteenth century throughout Islam and into the sixteenth century along the Varangian trade routes that followed the rivers from Persia and Byzantium through Russia and Sweden.

It was the latter type that was destined to accompany the game to
Europe. The graceful, abstract shapes of these pieces would fire the
imaginations of European artisans. There the game, and the pieces
with which it was played, would once again be transformed, reflecting
new cultures with different perspectives and needs from those of the
Arabs, Persians, and Indians before them.

CHAPTER THREE

THE ESTABLISHMENT OF THE GAME IN EUROPE

W HEN CHESS REACHED Europe, various types of board games were already being played by culturally diverse groups of people living throughout the continent. Among the games enjoyed were those inherited from classical antiquity such as merels (tic-tac-toe) and backgammon, as well as indigenous games played by the Norse, Germanic, or Celtic inhabitants of the North. As chess became popular in Europe, many of the latter games fell into disuse and eventually were forgotten. Some, such as the Welsh game of *gwyddbwyll* or the Irish game of *fidchell,* disappeared so completely that it is nearly impossible to reconstruct the play of the game. They survive only as literary references in collections of folk stories and legends.

Once introduced, chess caught on rapidly, especially among the

KING, ITALY, (CHARLEMAGNE CHESSMAN), IVORY, LATE 11TH–EARLY 12TH CENTURY

The set to which this king belongs may represent two opposing sides in the conflict between the leader of the Norman forces, Robert Guiscard (1014–1085) and Byzantine Emperor (and chess player) Alexis Comenus I (1048–1118). By 1061 Guiscard had ousted the Arabs from Sicily and parts of southern Italy. He then turned his attention toward the Byzantine Empire, throwing them out of Italy and pursuing them into Greece where shortly after his death, his forces were defeated.

35

ILLUMINATION, SPAIN, OPAQUE WATERCOLOR AND GOLD LEAF, 1283

This illumination, showing an Arab and Spaniard playing chess, is from the book, *Libros del axedrez, dados et tablas*. In Spain, the Arabs fostered a period of tolerance that even extended into nearby Christian kingdoms. Not only did Christians, Hebrews, and Arabs mix freely in this society, their ideas did as well. Alfonso X, the Christian King of Castile and León, also encouraged such relationships. He freely employed intellectuals of all backgrounds to write and translate books for his encyclopedic collection of knowledge. Not only was one of these books dedicated to chess and other games, but pastimes such as chess, would have been a natural way to extend friendships first made in this intellectual and cultural mix of people.

upper classes. Less clear is its popularity among the lower classes. Recent archaeological findings in Russia suggest that chess was widely played by various classes at least from the twelfth through the fifteenth century, but it is difficult to assess the popularity of the game among the working classes elsewhere in Europe. Although references to the game appear in the literature, household accounts, and wills of the elite, no such evidence exists for those living and working below them. Medieval society functioned because those living at the bottom supported those at the top. Given that the lower classes may not have had the luxury of time, they may have preferred to find their entertainment in less time-consuming pastimes such as dice or merels. Whether or not chess was commonly played by all levels of society, it quickly became closely associated with the aristocracy and gentry throughout the medieval period.

The earliest known European reference to the game, *Versus de scachis* (also called the *Einsiedeln Verses,* after the Swiss monastery where the manuscript is located), is a ninety-eight-line poem now dated sometime in the 990s. Because the subject of the poem is a game of chess, it suggests that chess must have been fairly well known—at least in southern Europe—before the end of the tenth century. If so, who was responsible for its introduction to its European admirers: the Arabs, who subjugated much of Spain and Sicily, or the Byzantine Empire, which controlled southern Italy and traded with the city-states of the North? And did it also travel on the longboats of Viking traders up the Volga River system of eastern Europe?

Este es otro iuego departido en que ha uey
nt τ anco tablas que an a seer entabla
dos assi como estan en la figura del entau
blamiento τ han se de iogar desta guisa.

Os blacos iuega primo τ dan
mate al rey preto en xi. ueze
de los sus iuegos en la segunda
casa del cauallo blanco. en
tre o esta el alfferza blanca

el rey preto: en la segunda casa de so al
fil. τ El quinto iuego dar la xaque con el
cauallo blanco. en la casa del rey preto. τ
entra el rey preto: en la segunda casa de so
cauallo. τ El serto iuego dar la xaque con
el cauallo blanco. en la casa del alfferza pre
ta. τ entra el rey preto: en la tercera casa
de so xaque. τ El sereno iuego dar la xaque
con el cauallo blanco. en la segunda casa

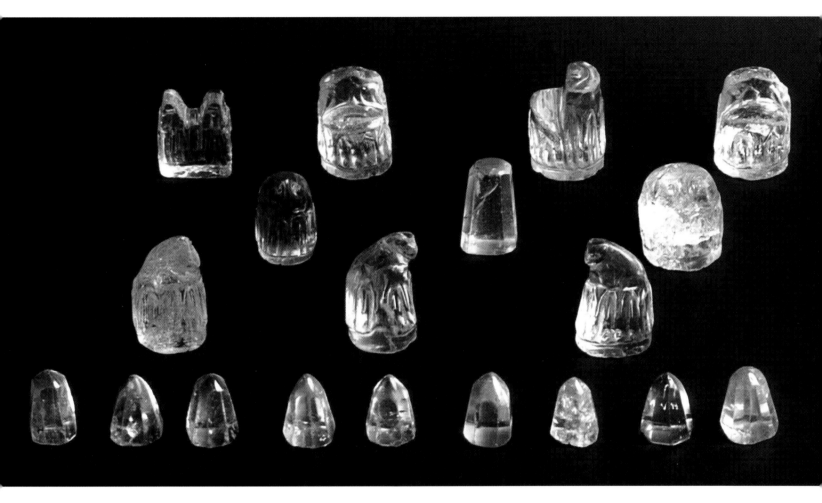

CHESS SET, ARAB-SPAIN, ROCK CRYSTAL, LATE 9TH–EARLY 11TH CENTURY

In demand for luxury items, rock crystal was mined in East Africa and the west coast of India and imported by Arab workshops specializing in it throughout the Arab Empire. These chess pieces, carved in the Arab style, were probably produced in a Spanish-Arab workshop. In Europe, rock crystal objects were often associated with saints and, as a result, were highly prized. Because of this mystique, pieces from rock crystal sets were sometimes used to embellish the reliquaries prized in church treasuries. Two surviving wills dating from the 11th century both mention rock crystal sets given to the parish church of Ager in Catalonia. The set illustrated here, now known as the Ager Chessmen, may be one or perhaps parts of both of these sets.

EARLY DAYS

The most likely agent for the spread of chess to Europe was the Arabs. Known to their new European neighbors as the Moors, in Spain, or the Saracens, in southern Italy and Sicily, Arabs had already occupied parts of southern Europe for nearly three centuries by the time the first mention of chess appears in European chronicles. Beginning in 711, with the political authority of the caliph of Damascus, Arabs quickly took control of nearly all of the Iberian Peninsula. In 756, Abd ar-Rahman I established an independent emirate there, and the caliphate of Córdoba was founded in 929 by his descendant and namesake Abd ar-Rahman III. The dynasty lasted until 1031, and under its influence Spain flourished, becoming a center of European intellectual activity. The caliphs were patrons of the arts and sciences, supporting an array of universities and schools, as well as other sophisticated pursuits. Chess, with its close intellectual associations, was very much a part of this world of academic exchange and curiosity. Indeed, the caliphs of Córdoba themselves indulged in the game, and their chroniclers reported on various feats and contests—including, for the first time in Europe, games of chess played blindfolded.

The joy of the game must have been quickly imparted to the Christian population of Spain. Undisputed references to chess date to the closing days of the caliphate of Córdoba. For example, the will of Ermengaud I, count of Urgel, written just prior to his death in battle against the Moors in 1008, left his chessmen to the convent of Saint-

Once Europeans became comfortable with the abstracted style of chessmen they inherited from the Arabs, they began to elaborate and embellish their surfaces but still retained the basic form and shape of the Arabic pieces. Here, superimposed on the surface is a carved relief presenting an image of a king and two members of his court under a ceremonial archway.

Gilles near Nîmes, France. About fifty years later, his sister-in-law Countess Ermessind, widow of the count of Barcelona, left a rock-crystal set to Saint-Gilles as well. (The rock-crystal set portrayed on page 38 traditionally associated with the count of Urgel, the so-called Ager Chessmen, survives today in the diocesan museum at Lleida, Spain.) Later, one of the earliest European books on chess was written under the supervision of Alfonso X, known as Alfonso the Wise (reigned 1252–1284), the Christian king of Castile and León. Completed by 1283, the *Libros del axedrez, dados et tablas* features more than a hundred chess problems, with corresponding illustrations.

Besides Spain, the Arabs also had significant influence over southern Italy and Sicily. Originally they went ashore to assist rebels fighting against the political dominance of the Byzantine Empire. Instead, they conquered, subjugating Sicily by 827 and exerting influence over southern Italy through established outposts thereafter. They exercised power over the region until the latter part of the eleventh century, when the Normans expelled both the Arabs and the Byzantine Empire from southern Italy and Sicily. It seems clear that the Arabs may have introduced the game into southern Italy about the same time it was introduced into Spain.

Not only does the physical and literary evidence support the hypothesis that chess was introduced to southern Europe by the Arabs, but so does some of the vocabulary of the game. Although the process is tangled, the nomenclature of chess found in most European language groups was largely translated or derived from Arabic, some-

times through the intermediary of Latin. For example, the name of the game, chess (*échecs* in French, *Schach* in German, and *scachus* in Latin), came from the Arabic word for shah. Some European piece names retained the same or similar meaning to the Arabic term: *shah* was translated as king; *faras* (horse) as knight; and the *baidaq* (footman) became pawn. Others had a more dramatic change. Perhaps because it was a natural European pairing with the king, the term *firzan* (vizier or Wiseman) transformed to queen. Since the meaning of the Arabic term *al-fil* (elephant) was not always understood, Europeans extrapolated names from the physical presence of the piece. Thus the pointed projections (tusks) of the piece suggested the miters, hats, and caps of bishops, judges, and fools. Interestingly, one Arabic term, *rukh*, survived virtually intact (as the Latin *rochus*) and eventually appeared in English as the word *rook*, even though the meaning changed by then from "chariot" to "castle."

Less of a case can be made for the role that the Byzantine Empire may have played in the European adoption of chess. Plainly, that empire enjoyed the game at an early date, acquiring it from Arab-Persian sources sometime well before the beginning of the tenth century. It is less clear if chess was as popular a pastime in the Byzantine Empire as it was in the neighboring Arab world. However, the game did have noted enthusiasts. Anna Comnena, the author of a biographical work about her father, Emperor Alexius I Comnenus (reigned 1081–1118), wrote that he played chess for relaxation.

Given that the Byzantine Empire maintained control of southern

KNIGHT,
FRENCH,
IVORY,
12TH CENTURY

European artists gradually covered the surface of the Arab-style pieces so completely that the stories depicted in the reliefs dominated its form and shape. In this figure, the energy comes from the deeply carved reliefs of two knights battling as they race around the form. Here the artist almost, but not quite, obliterates the older Arabic model.

The image of or term for a boat to represent the rook is used by different groups of people throughout Asia. More than likely its use simply reflects different cultural interpretations of what the older Arabic chariot piece actually represented. The Russians must have seen a similarity in the shape and form of the Arabic rook to the trading vessels they used to ply the rivers and inland seas, and began calling it *ladya*, or boat. Once identified with a boat, Russian carvers elaborated upon the design of the rook until centuries later it took on the appearance of a 17th-century frigate. The rook is also represented by the word *boat*, or its image, in western India, Thailand, Bangladesh, and parts of Indonesia.

Italy from the fall of the Roman Empire in 476 until the Norman conquest in the eleventh century, it is possible that chess arrived in Europe from there. However, if chess was a Byzantine gift to Europe, little evidence exists of that legacy. At the very least, the nomenclature of the game should reflect some Greek Byzantine influence, and it does not.

More of a case can be made that chess traveled up the Dnieper and Volga river systems, along the Varangians' trade routes from the Byzantine Empire to Sweden, as early as the tenth and eleventh centuries. Since the ninth century, Scandinavian settlers and traders, or Vikings, had inhabited the interior of eastern Europe, where they united the Kievan Rus (now Ukraine, Belarus, and parts of Russia) under the house of Rurik in 882, beginning a seven-hundred-year dynasty. The Rus traded at Constantinople and at Baghdad from the ninth through the eleventh century.

Chess apparently traveled north into Russia and eastern Europe from Baghdad at approximately the same time it arrived in Spain and southern Italy. Recognizable playing pieces stylistically related to early Arab models have recently been discovered at archaeological sites near Kiev, Novgorod, and other early Russian towns, suggesting that the game was widely known there by the eleventh century, and probably much earlier. The etymology of the Russian nomenclature of the game indicates that it was derived from Arabic rather than Greek, suggesting that the game was inherited from the Arabs, either bypassing or simply traveling through the Byzantine Empire into the interior of eastern Europe. The Russian word for chess, *shakmaty*, is derived from the Arabic *shatranj*, while terms for the playing pieces were either direct translations or adapted from Arabic. As in the West, when the Russians had difficulty understanding the meaning behind the name of a particular playing piece, they simply imposed a known cultural icon over the unknown name. For example, in Russia the name for the rook became *lad'ia* or *ladya*, meaning "boat." To the Russians, the Arab playing piece may have resembled the Russian boats commonly plying the Dnieper, Volga, and Don rivers of the region.

It would seem, then, that chess existed in Russia and eastern Europe at an early date, introduced to the region at about the same time that it spread to western Europe by emissaries of the Arab Empire. Indeed, Arab influence on chess in Europe cannot be underestimated. It was the Arabs, not the Byzantines, who played the dominant role in the spread of the game to their European neighbors before the turn of the millennium. Chess arrived in Europe along with Greek classical literature, science, arithmetic, and other disciplines of the ancient world in the amassed knowledge of the Arabs, generously shared with their European neighbors. Still, as Arab influence began to decline, it would be the Europeans who would play the dominant role over the next millennium, adapting and changing the game of chess forever. Under the care of the Europeans, chess would flourish.

EARLY EUROPEAN PLAYING PIECES

The earliest European playing pieces were based on an abstract style that the Arabs developed from the earlier representational design of the Persians. One of the oldest examples may be those known as the San Sebastian Chessmen, so called because they were found in the San Sebastian Catacombs in Rome. The catacombs were used for burials until the fourth or fifth century and remained a pilgrimage site well into the medieval period. The chess pieces found have been dated as early as the seventh century. If true, it would push back the date for the introduction of the game into Europe. However, the pieces could have been left as an offering even as late as the eleventh century. Similarly styled sets have been dated to the end of the ninth, tenth, and even eleventh centuries.

Surviving chess pieces from the late tenth century show evidence that European artisans were already tentatively experimenting with the older Arab model. Following the lead of Arab craftsmen before them, they inscribed circular motifs in decorative patterns and borders around individual pieces, and they occasionally added eyes to the knight (horse). With growing assurance, they began to embellish the entire surface of each piece. Surviving European rock-crystal sets, most likely made in workshops in Arab-controlled Spain, are characterized by curvilinear or geometric patterns enriching the surfaces but retaining the basic form and shape of each piece.

European artists toyed with the surfaces of the forms in this

ROOK, ITALY, IVORY, LATE 11TH CENTURY

This atypical piece of the period heralds a new age in chess design in Europe. It completely leaves behind the abstracted rook image of the Arab model, and proposes a new model based on architecture. It is perhaps one of the earliest European expressions of the rook as castle. Yet the shape is still a support for the reliefs which infuse the surface with energy and life.

47

ROOK, FRENCH, IVORY, 12TH CENTURY

As late as the 12th century, the Arabic model could still dominate the form and shape of chess pieces. Carved in deep relief on one side of this small rook is the image of two knights sparring in combat. On the other side, Adam, Eve, and the Tree of Knowledge fill the surface. Like most surviving medieval chessmen, this piece, once gilded, would have been part of a set made for someone of high rank.

fashion until the beginning of the eleventh century. Then, comfortable with representational imagery (unlike the Arabs), they began to overlay the simple, elegant forms and shapes of the older model with intricately carved relief images. Like the Romanesque style that influenced them, the exterior of each piece became richly and ornately embellished with figures, architectural details, and tracery. Christian and classical imagery graced the surfaces. Figures might be placed within architectural settings—in rooms, under arches, or behind flowing curtains. Over the course of the century, artists continued to manipulate the surface, deeply piercing and carving them until the older Arab form and shape became unrecognizable.

By the time the European nomenclature of the game was established in the twelfth century, certain motifs had become associated with the names of individual pieces. As noted earlier, in some cases Europeans used words influenced by the Arabic terms for the pieces: *shah* was easily translated to refer to the king, while the horse became the knight. As European terms became established they began to suggest images to artisans throughout the continent. The pawn, recognized as the least of the pieces, was diversely represented as foot soldiers, as peasants, or even, as in the case of the Lewis Chessmen, as stones or grave markers. However, the names for the elephant, chariot, and vizier had no real European equivalent. Instead, Europeans compared the shapes of the pieces to what they knew. Thus, the abstracted elephant, with its projections representing tusks, suggested a bishop's miter to some and a fool's cap to others. In western Europe, the

BISHOP, QUEEN, ROOK (LEWIS CHESSMEN), SCANDINAVIA, WALRUS IVORY, LATE 12TH CENTURY

In the late 12th century a merchant stashed four chess sets and other trade items in a hole on the Isle of Lewis, in the Outer Hebrides of Scotland. He never returned for his treasure. Perhaps he was lost at sea or died in some conflict elsewhere. Ironically, the uncertainty and hardship of his life and that of others living in the 12th century, is beautifully conveyed in the sadness and even weariness that these miniature figures express. This quality and the three-dimensionality of these pieces, mark a turning point in the way Europeans presented chess figures. As the 13th century begins, three-dimensional, representational chessmen begin to appear throughout Europe, leaving the Arab model completely behind.

rukh (chariot) suggested a castle tower, while in Russia it was sometimes represented by a bird, but more commonly a boat. In the West, Europeans discarded the concept of a vizier and designated the piece as a queen; in the East, the piece was variously represented as a female or a male. As artists struggled to present images representing the subject of each piece, they increasingly violated the line and form of the older Arab model, until it no longer existed.

THE CHARLEMAGNE AND LEWIS CHESSMEN

Two sets, carved nearly a century apart, dramatically characterize the transformation of the Arabic chess play pieces into distinct European interpretations and forms during the twelfth century. The first of these, known as the Charlemagne Chessmen (legends associate them with the popular French king and Holy Roman Emperor) were actually carved in southern Italy in the late eleventh, or opening decades of the twelfth centuries (pictured on pages 15, 29, and 35). Although the presentation of the kings and queens suggest the form and shape of the Arabic playing pieces, the other figures are carved in the round, leaving the older model behind. The subjects represented (queens, chariots, and elephants) and the stylistic characteristics of the pieces, showed strong influences from the Arab, Byzantium and European cultures mixing so freely in southern Italy at the time.

The so-called Lewis Chessmen were probably carved in a Scandinavian workshop and carried by a merchant traveling from Norway to

Ireland sometime in the late twelfth century. They were stashed for unknown reasons on the Isle of Lewis where they were found in 1831. Recovered from the site were seventy-eight chessmen, nearly four complete sets. In looking at them, it is abundantly clear that not only are the Lewis Chessmen realistically carved in the round, departing from the forms and shapes of the old Arab model, but more importantly, they present a completely European conceptualization of the playing pieces. Included among the pieces are clearly recognizable European kings, queens, bishops, knights, and rooks. From this point on, European artists would know no limitations to the form and style of the playing pieces. The Arab model was, to all intents and purposes, gone from Europe.

CHAPTER FOUR
MODELLING THE UNIVERSE

A S CHESS FIGURES BECAME more three-dimensional and expressive, the game itself became symbolically, intellectually, and socially important throughout Europe, spilling over into many other aspects of medieval art and culture. Vignettes of players appear in numerous illuminated manuscripts, as well as on small decorative and functional objects of the time. The histories of the day frequently allude to the game, and in literature the great courtly romances describe heroes and lovers who play chess. Educators encouraged the game, often listing it as an important accomplishment of the learned lady or knight. Works of morality and theology went a step further, often employing the game as a metaphor for weightier matters. Beyond question, the game's greatest appeal was that it was almost instantly recognized as a microcosm of society. Medieval intellectuals, constantly engaged in creating models of the universe that surrounded them, saw chess, with its kings and queens, knights and bishops, castles and pawns, as an obvious paradigm.

Jacobus de Cessolis, a Lombard friar, wrote one of the most popular works along these lines. Titled the *Liber de moribus hominum et*

MIRROR, FRENCH, IVORY, C. 1320-40

By the 14th century, chess had become a favorite motif with writers and artists who used its imagery and drama to enrich popular courtly themes. One of these was love. As a consequence, lovers were commonly pictured playing chess. Featured here on the ivory case of a small hand-held mirror, is a relief of a couple playing chess. It was fashionable for the ladies of the court to carry mirrors, like this one, representing courtly themes.

Between 1280 and 1320, a
Lombard friar by the name
of Jacobus de Cessolis,
wrote one of the most
popular books of the
medieval period, *Liber de
moribus hominum et officiis
nobilium*. In the book,
Cessolis recorded a sermon
originally written to
"correct the evil manners
of the king, avoid idleness
and sadness and satisfy the
natural desire for novelty
by means of the infinite
variety of play," and used
the game of chess as an
allegory for medieval life.
In Cessolis's book, the
chessboard represents
the city of Babylon, and
the pieces represent kings,
queens, knights, and
judges or legates. Pawns
are presented as members
of any number of trades
and professions of the day.

r lita eert laepuic et ptieç ftatuut an

His playe fonde a phylosopher of thoryent

t was named in caldee Exerses or in greke
for which is as moche to say in englissh as he th
Justyce and mesure / And this philosopher was
gretly among the grekes and them of Athene
were good clerkys and phylosophers also renome
connyng / This philosopher was so Just and tre
had leuer dye / than to lyue longe and be a fal
with the sayd kyng / For whan he behelde the fo
ful lyf of the kyng · And that no man durst bl

He causes Wherfore this playe was founden ben iij

t · The first was for to correcte and repreue the kyng
for whan this kyng enylmerodach sawe this playe / And
the bawns · knyghtes and gentilmen of his court playe
wyth the phylosopher, he merueylled gretly of the beaulte
and noueltee of the playe · And desired to playe agaynst
the philosopher / The philosopher answerd and sayd to hym
that hit myght not be don / but yf he first lernyd the play
The kyng sayd hit was reson and that he wold put hym
to the payn to lerne hit / Than the phylosopher began to

56

officiis nobilium (Book of the Customs of Men and the Duties of Nobles), and written between 1280 and 1320, it portrayed chess as a symbol of society, its ranks and degrees reflecting the fate of humankind. Just as each playing piece has its proper place and station, it states, so too does each member of society have an appropriate role to play. To emphasize the point, Cessolis even vividly described each pawn as representing a different occupation of the time. More importantly, however, as he developed his theme it became clear that all the pieces—and by inference all members of medieval society—were interdependent. In effect, Cessolis was implying that the king was as dependent on the lesser ranks as they were on him—a profound idea with great appeal among the intellectuals of the era. Consequently, the *Liber de moribus hominum et officiis nobilium* became extremely popular, and it continued to be published well into the next century. More than eighty versions have been preserved in Latin alone. Dozens of translations in several other European languages also exist, including the English edition, *The Game and Playe of the Chesse,* published by William Caxton in 1480. The remarkable number of copies that have survived is strongly indicative of its powerful attraction to the medieval mind.

ILLUSTRATIONS, ENGLAND, WOODCUT, 1480

Cessolis's book on chess was so popular that literally dozens of copies survive to the present day. The first printed edition in English, *The Game and Playe of the Chesse,* was produced by the printer William Caxton in Brussels in 1474. A second edition containing a number of extraordinary woodcuts like these here, was printed by Caxton in England in 1480 under the sign of the Red Pale at Westminster. In the woodcut on the left the main character of the book, the Philosopher, prepares to discuss chess. In the second, he teaches the king to play.

A COURTLY ACCOMPLISHMENT

Further evidence of the popularity of chess can be found in the fashionable romance genre of the period, in which chess was often used as a literary convention to further the plot of the tale. In these stories, chess is routinely portrayed as the catalyst for bringing

ILLUMINATION,
FRENCH,
OPAQUE
WATERCOLOR,
14TH CENTURY

This manuscript illumination from a version of the story of Tristan and Isolde depicts the moment in which the ill-fated lovers accidently drink a love potion meant for King Mark and Isolde to drink at their wedding. In this scene, they drink the potion while playing chess and soon fall madly in love with each other. The story ends with Tristan's banishment from court.

star-crossed lovers together. Among the most famous of them are Tristan and Isolde, and Lancelot and Guinevere. But skill at chess was also considered a crucial attribute of the great heroes of medieval fiction, such as King Arthur and the French champion Roland. Indeed, the association of greatness with the ability to play chess encouraged chroniclers to give noted historical figures from the past a larger-than-life skill at the game. For example, Charlemagne, the famous king of the Franks (reigned 742–814) and emperor of the West (reigned 800–814), was often attributed with enormous skill at the game—though it is highly unlikely he even knew of it. Later chroniclers, believing that his stature demanded such skill, reported that he not only played with great ability but also owned several admirable sets.

The famous were not the only ones linked to the game. The courtly tradition espoused by the troubadours in their romances and ballads was mirrored in the numerous advice books written about the necessary accomplishments for learned women and men of the day. A gentlewoman was admonished that her education was not complete until she learned to hawk, tell stories, sing and play instruments, read and write, and play chess with competence. The ability to play well became so closely linked to the idea of the heroic champion that Petrus Alfonsi listed it as one of the seven knightly accomplishments (along with riding, swimming, archery, boxing, hawking, and verse writing) in his early-twelfth-century book titled the *Disciplina Clericalis.*

Moreover, the everyday world of the well-to-do was infused with images of chess. Closely identified as it was with courtly accomplish-

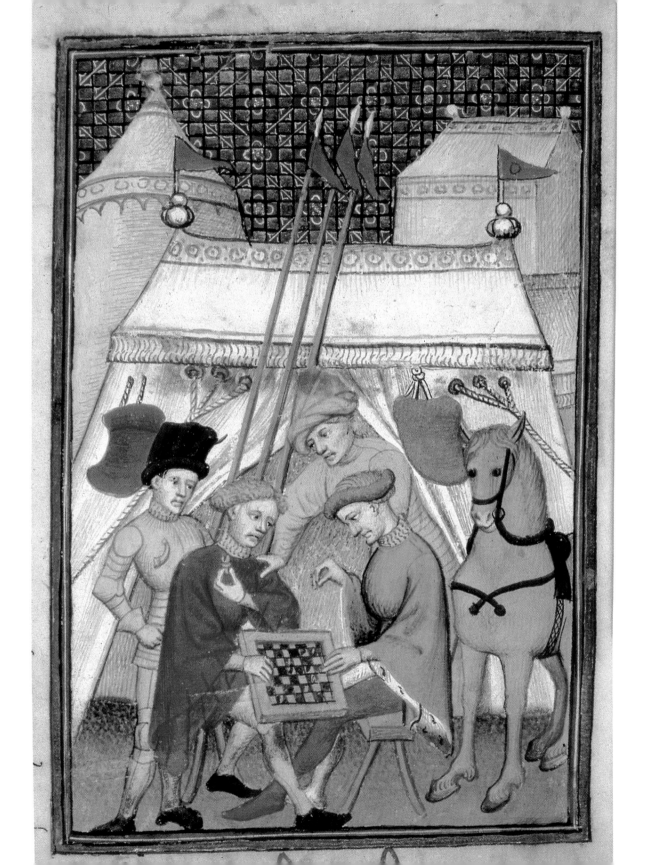

ments, chess quickly became important as a status symbol, and consequently chess sets had a place of honor in most upper-class households. Not only were there sets and boards in all the great houses, but chess was a popular motif appearing in works of art from the twelfth through the fourteenth centuries. Illuminated books, tapestries, and carved reliefs on everything from cathedrals and reliquaries to such commonplace items as mirrors all portrayed tableaux of people playing chess. That chess was perceived as significant, at least among the upper classes, is also amply recorded in wills, legal records, household inventories, and other historical documents of the period.

Although the image of chess certainly lent itself to popular consumption among the well-to-do, there were also a limited number of players who were serious about the game, even if their standards were never high. It was the more impassioned players who, over time, proposed a number of limited technical changes to the game. These included advancing the pawns by two squares instead of one at the start of the game and empowering the kings and queens to leap squares. These changes not only speeded up the game but gave it more flexibility and interest in play. A number of "problem books" were written to describe these new innovations, game positions, and methods of play. Although existing manuscripts date only from the thirteenth century, more than likely they had existed for some time—perhaps initially traveling with the game when it was inherited from the Arabs centuries earlier. The earliest of these include the *Bonus Socius*, compiled before 1300, and the previously mentioned manuscript of King Alfonso the Wise of 1283.

ILLUMINATION, FRENCH, OPAQUE WATERCOLOR AND GOLD LEAF, C. 1410–1415

Images of chess were often used by writers and illuminators to enhance the courtly flavor of a story or illustration. In this illumination characters from one of the stories in *The Book of the City of Ladies* by Christine de Pizan (1364–1430?) play chess between jousts at a tournament. The book was originally written in 1405, and was an account of the heroic deeds of women. At the age of twenty-four, Frenchwoman Christine de Pizan found herself widowed and penniless. In order to reverse her fortunes, she took up the pen and began to write courtly romances, poems, and other forms of literature.

Medieval chess was a long, and at times tedious game. It was not uncommon for a game to last for days, as play was complex and slow. In addition, although chess was portrayed as intellectual, idealistic, romantic, and even heroic in literature and art, there was a seamier side to it throughout the medieval period: chess easily lent itself to gambling. Gambling added interest to the game, and indeed court records in both England and France document losses and gains at chess, while some books on the game also include strategies for cheating on wagers. It will come as no surprise that the church took umbrage at this activity, and it made periodic attempts to censor the game.

CHESS AND THE CHURCH

Even though chess was probably first spread by the European clergy, it acquired its share of religious detractors almost from the moment it first appeared on that continent. The Western church objected to the game on many different occasions, banning clergy from playing chess at various times throughout the eleventh until as late as the thirteenth century. In fact, one of the earliest historical references to chess in Europe is in a letter to Pope Alexander II from Peter Damian, cardinal bishop of Ostia (later declared a saint), who wrote in 1061 that he had been forced to impose a penitence on a bishop who played chess.

Like the Arab religious leaders before them, the European clergy felt that too much attention was being given to a game that was

BISHOP, GERMAN, IVORY, 14TH CENTURY

By the 14th century, representational chess pieces had become highly embellished and extremely ornamental. Chess figures, such as the bishop shown here, were often depicted as a central figure with their retinue surrounding them. The smaller figures were less important than larger ones. In the case of this bishop, he is attended by five clerks and a troop of bowmen holding crossbows. The latter were known as a *glaive* or *sword* of men.

KING,
DANISH,
IVORY,
14TH CENTURY

With his extraordinary, sad visage staring back at us, a king rides forth upon a lion. He is accompanied by an attendant (his smaller size a reflection of his lesser rank) holding a spear and shield emblazoned with a dragon. The 14th-century artisan who made this beautiful chess piece took great pains in accurately portraying details such as the chain mail, weapons, helmet, and padded tunic of this warrior-king. The use of the lion as a mount for a royal person is an early example of a motif that would be more commonly used in the 16th century.

largely frivolous and, worse, had become associated with gambling. The game was forbidden in the rule book of the Knights Templar (1128–1153); and censored bishops and clerical assemblies included the Council of Paris in 1202; Eudes of Sully, bishop of Paris, in 1208; the Provincial Synod of 1255; and the Council of Trier in 1310. In 1254, King Louis IX attempted to ban the game among not only the clergy but also the general population of France. However, in the West the anti-chess sentiment within the church was losing the battle. Not only did members of the clergy play the game, it was popular among the upper ranks of medieval society. Loath to offend its rich patrons, and somewhat ineffectual in preventing its own members from playing the game, the minority of clergy opposed to the game were finding it difficult to sustain an effective ban. In the end, church censorship had little or no real impact on the popularity of the game in Western Europe. Indeed, paradoxically it was the church itself—the repository of learning and intellectual activity—which helped to spread the game throughout Western Europe.

On the other hand, the Orthodox Church in the East, equally concerned with what it considered the demoralizing effects that the game was having on its constituents, was somewhat more effective. Beginning in the twelfth century, it repeatedly banned chess, and, unlike its counterpart in the West, it continued to do so up until the eighteenth century. Perhaps because chess had never achieved the social prestige in the East to the extent that it had in the West, the Orthodox Church was able to effect more of a change, at least outwardly. Fewer images, motifs, and stories about chess appear in works of art and courtly literature in the East, and little was written about the game, its history, the players, or game problems and solutions. Nevertheless, in spite of the edicts, the physical evidence of chess pieces recovered from archaeological sites from the period, as well as the appearance of the game in popular Russian legends and stories, attests to a widespread general interest in the game. Indeed, the game may have enjoyed broader status among the general population in Eastern Europe than it did in the West.

KNIGHT, ENGLISH, WALRUS IVORY, 13TH CENTURY

This piece, with traces of its original gilding and color, strongly suggests that chess pieces made throughout the 12th, 13th, and into the 14th centuries were often lavishly decorated. Together with the other thirty-one pieces that would have comprised this set, it must have made an impressive display—fit for the king or nobleman for whom it most likely was intended.

MEDIEVAL CHESSMEN

Throughout the thirteenth and fourteenth centuries, chess pieces continued to evolve into complex three-dimensional objects that could stand as miniature sculptures in their own right. The abstract forms and shapes of the older Arab models completely disappeared. Playing pieces became diminutive figures of kings, queens, bishops, knights, castles, and pawns. Surviving sets from the period reveal figures that grasp robes, crosiers, swords, reins, and birds, while others play horns, raise their hands in a blessing, or point. Queens might be shown as court ladies on caparisoned mounts, while knights on horseback are portrayed throwing spears or drawing their swords out of their scabbards. Pawns, portrayed as foot soldiers, march forward with swords and shields raised. Everywhere, movement is suggested. The pieces are rarely static.

Late medieval playing pieces illustrate the intense relationships between the social classes of medieval society. The largest and most impressive pieces are the king and queen, followed by the bishop, knight, and so on. This was perhaps best expressed in the fondness for elaboration and decorative detail in late-fourteenth-century pieces from northern Europe. There the individual playing pieces were beautifully portrayed and surrounded by retinues of smaller people: warriors, clergy, or members of the court. Some late medieval examples had two or three tiers of people encircling the dominant figure. The implication is as clear as the model that Cessolis proposed: everyone had his or her own place and sphere, but in the words of the poet John Donne, no man was an island. The universe was interconnected.

Because most sets were made for the well-to-do, European craftspeople could choose from a wide variety of materials. They included elephant ivory, walrus ivory, bone, rock crystal, jasper, amber, and ebony, as well as various hardwoods. Perhaps for its beauty and the ease with which it was worked, ivory was the most admired. Once a piece was finished, it was sometimes gilded, embellished with precious metals and gems, or painted.

THE CONVENTIONAL STYLE

Sophisticated and expensive sets were best suited for exhibition, not for play. Beautiful as they were, they were too valuable and fragile to be used every day. In addition, their size, form, and protruding elements, such as tiny swords or spears, made them awkward when used, impeding the progress of the game. Serious players needed simpler, more functional playing pieces. Further, as chess made its way down the social ladder to the burgeoning middle class, sets needed to be more readily obtainable and less costly.

Accordingly, craftspeople began to produce a conventional style of playing pieces made of simplified or abstracted shapes. Sets made of inexpen-

CHESS SET, SCANDINAVIA BONE, 14TH CENTURY

Few playing pieces, and fewer playing sets, made in the conventional style, either hand-carved or turned on a lathe—like this one—survived to the present day. They were, after all, inexpensive and meant to be used for play. Consequently, they were easily misplaced and lost over time. Fortunately, the popularity of the game insured that a record of their forms and shapes would remain—left on the carved and painted surfaces of luxury items and in the numerous illuminations and, later, printed illustrations found in hundreds of books written and printed throughout the period.

sive materials, such as bone or wood, were carved or turned on a lathe at a reasonable cost. As workhorses of the game, these playing pieces had little value, and were less likely to survive than their more expensive cousins. Consequently, few actual sets in this style have survived. Fortunately, frequent examples can be found in the illuminated and printed manuscripts of the period. Indeed, since few if any representational sets are illustrated in manuscripts of the time, conventional-style sets may have been more common than might be supposed by the evidence of surviving physical examples. Recent excavations of twelfth-, thirteenth-, and fourteenth-century sites along the Volga and Dnieper rivers suggest that playing sets of the conventional style were quite common, at least in eastern and northern Europe. The chessmen found are simple, handcarved or lathe-turned pieces made from bone or wood. Some of them were obviously inspired by the older Arabic abstract tradition.

Surviving pieces and manuscript illustrations demonstrate that although conventionally styled sets were based on the older Arab model first introduced into Europe, they quickly took on a distinctly European flavor. In many cases, the designs of playing pieces were determined by the lathe on which they were made. Many are completely schematic, with little hint of representation or subject. Like their Arab lathe-turned counterparts, these conventional pieces were often distinguished from one another mainly by height, width, and color. They might also be decorated with inscribed lines—some thin and others cut deeply into the material—to create undulating

PAWN, SHAH, VIZIER, TWO KNIGHTS AND A ROOK,
ARAB, ROCK CRYSTAL, SMOKEY TOPAZ AND GOLD FOIL, 13TH CENTURY

It is important to remember that while Europeans quickly assimilated the game of chess, making it their own, the game was still played by Muslims in much the same way that they had played it for centuries. Although they began using lathe-turned sets, they continued to use the traditional abstract model as playing pieces at least through the 13th century, and possibly longer. As they traveled further afield, they carried the game with them to parts of the African continent, and into Asia.

ridges and curves, up and down the trunk of each piece. Occasionally, a horse head or the double-headed rook might be carved by hand.

Before the thirteenth century, alterations to the game had been largely visual, but play remained agonizingly slow. Limited attempts to speed it up had resulted in the development of variants that briefly existed in pockets throughout Europe. But because the game was primarily a social phenomenon imbued with prestige and status, technical innovations in play largely went unnoticed. By the end of the thirteenth century, however, there was mounting pressure to speed up the game. The world was changing. People were no longer content to spend their leisure time listening to accounts of courtly romances and playing long games of chess. Chess had to adapt or it would be left behind.

vrouwen. daar men nochtan goede exem
pele bi mach verstaen ende leren.

At
mee
de
qua
et dat
een
heer
aen
hem
heb
ben
ma
ch is
als
hi go
des
niet

en . ontsiet. ende voir den menschen
hem niet en scaemt. voir gode zond vrese

CHAPTER FIVE
SPEEDING UP
THE GAME

THE IDEA OF SPEEDING UP the game seems to have spontaneously sprung up simultaneously throughout Europe sometime during the latter half of the fifteenth century. It almost seems to have been a universal concern. Why European players at this time wanted to change a game that had been played essentially the same way since they had inherited it from the Arabs centuries earlier is perplexing. It may have had its impetus in the larger, more complex developments that had taken place in European society.

The plague called The Black Death (1347–1351) and the Hundred Years War (1337–1453) transformed European culture forever, forcing extensive social and economic changes beginning in the latter part of the fourteenth century. While one event reduced the labor force in a drastic and horrific manner, the other, longer lasting and equally grisly with its scorched-earth military policies, disrupted the commercial system of France and its neighbors. As Europe slowly came out from under these devastating events, the older medieval order seemed

ILLUMINATION, OPAQUE WATERCOLOR AND GOLD LEAF, C. 1400–1410

Pictured, surrounded by their children, are a king and queen enjoying a game of chess. It is a detail of an illumination from a manuscript titled *Tafel van der Kerstenre Ghelove: Somerstuc* written by Dirc van Delf for the purpose of instructing the reader on a number of subjects, from the Passion and Ascension of Christ to the secular history and government of the Netherlands. In the latter, a chapter is devoted to acceptable games and pastimes for lords and ladies of the court, including the popular game of chess.

CHESSBOARD, FRENCH, WOOD AND IVORY, 15TH CENTURY

The ideal pastimes of the typical European court of the 15th century—the joust, music, dancing, and banquets—is presented in relief around the perimeter of this elegant board. Boards like this one were not only used for chess, but might also be displayed as wall decoration.

out-of-date. During the next few centuries as European society passed through the Renaissance and into the modern world, there were enormous challenges and accomplishments. This was the age of Copernicus, Galileo, and later Newton, who offered new insights into the workings of the physical universe, while explorers such as Columbus and Vasco da Gama expanded the boundaries of the known world. Elsewhere, the consequences of Martin Luther's challenge to the Catholic Church resulted in the Protestant Reformation, leading to decades of violent conflict before an uneasy tolerance for diverse beliefs within the Christian community became established. Intellectuals such as Erasmus and Thomas More examined humanist philosophical matters, while artists such as Leonardo da Vinci and writers such as Shakespeare explored both the inner workings of humankind and the natural world. Although these and other significant developments themselves had little or no direct impact on chess itself, its long-standing association with intellectual activity and learning suggests that the game must have been very much a part of this sophisticated mixture. Indeed, in this period of reexamination and inquiry, it is surprising not that chess underwent a major transformation, but that it survived at all.

Modifications to the game were not without precedent. Variations of chess had been played throughout the late medieval period. By the end of the fifteenth century, however, some variants had become widely accepted, dramatically affecting the way the game was universally played. Most significant were the changes made in the manner in

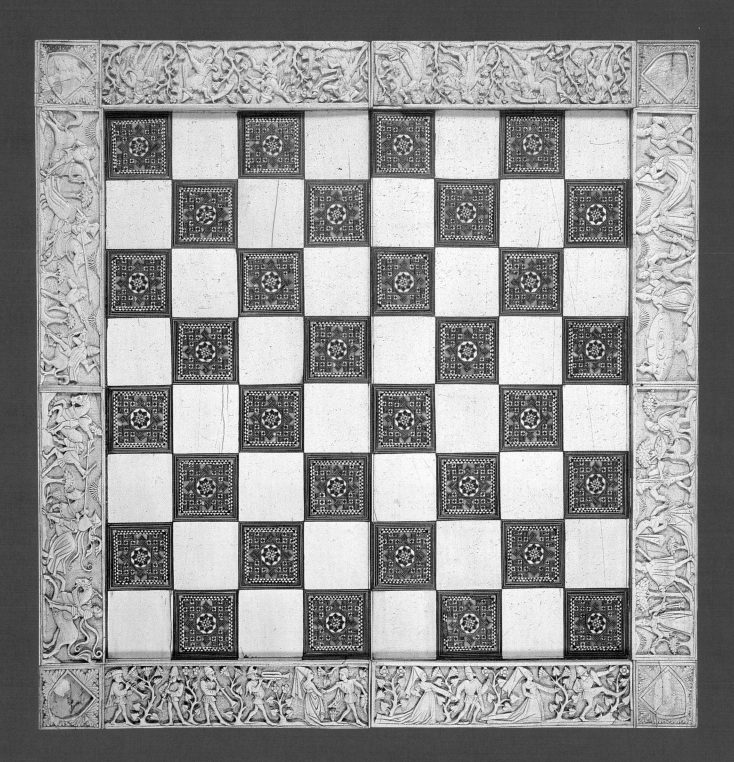

QUEEN, GERMAN, PAINTED IVORY, 16TH CENTURY

By the 16th century, chess pieces began to present fantastic figures based on literary and pictorial accounts of explorers. And what these sources lacked was more then adequately supplemented by the human imagination. This queen, dressed in a European interpretation of Arab clothing, rides a lion sidesaddle, a popular motif found in sets of the century. By the time this piece was carved, the queen could move diagonally, horizontally, and vertically, crossing as many squares as was desired or until she was forced to take another piece. This new rule not only made the queen the most powerful playing piece on the board, but served to speed up the game, and help transform it into the game played today.

which the bishop and the queen were deployed. The bishop, previously allowed to move only one square at a time, was suddenly given the ability to move diagonally over several squares on each move. This gave the piece as much power as the rook, which could move vertically or horizontally over several squares at a time. Even more important were the changes associated with the queen. Suddenly, and without any apparent cause, the queen could now move over multiple squares in any direction at a time, making it the most powerful piece in the game. Such was the shift in the emphasis of the game that for a time it was called the Queen's Chess.

Significantly, these new rule changes allowed a player to engage the opponent almost immediately, forcing the play to move forward at a much more rapid pace. In old chess, as the older version came to be called, a player could sit back and lay siege, slowly developing strategies for winning. Suddenly, players no longer had the luxury of time if they wanted to win the game. Checkmate could and did happen in the opening moments of the game. By the end of the fifteenth century these reforms, initially instituted to quicken the game, had instead completely remade it, transforming chess into a near twin of the game played today.

Although pinpointing exactly where, and even when, this new game originated is difficult; it is generally believed that it developed somewhere in southern Europe. This is hardly surprising, as it was the South where chess was first established in Europe. Sustained play over several centuries allowed ample time for variations to develop and take root. Evidence, drawn largely from the "problem books" in which the new game was discussed, suggests that it began sometime between 1470 and 1490 in Italy, Spain, and southern France.

The first of these books, published in Salamanca, Spain, in 1496 or 1497 and titled *Repeticion de amores e arte de axedrez (Discourse on Love and Art of Chess)*, brought together two unrelated treatises, the first on courtship and the other on chess problems involving the new innovations. In the book, the Spanish author, Luis de Lucena, writes that much of his material was collected in Italy and parts of France. Interestingly, the work devotes as much space to the old as the new form of play, suggesting that both were equally popular. Lucena's book was followed by others exploring and expanding upon the reforms, and within three decades after its publication the old game had disappeared.

Despite renewed interest in the game as an intellectual activity, chess gradually underwent a shift in its audience and faced stiff com-

petition from other popular leisure-time activities. Members of the upper classes could choose from other board games, various card games, singing, dancing, and theater to fill their free time. Indeed, advice books no longer mentioned chess as a skill necessary for success. Young men were even advised by Baldassare Castiglione, in his 1528 work the *Libro del cortegiano (Book of the Courtier)*, that although the game was a "pleasing and ingenious amusement," their time could be better spent on more profitable endeavors. Perhaps the powers of concentration needed to play the new game was a stumbling block to its popularity. Nevertheless, something of its cachet remained, and it continued to be considered a genteel occupation, with most households owning a chess set and board, if only as a status symbol.

While the upper classes were becoming disenchanted with chess as a leisure activity, the expanding intellectual elite of Europe were growing ever more absorbed by the game. Over time, chess came to be regarded as an activity requiring great intellectual skill. Players became recognized for their abilities, and competition became fiercer.

THE HEROIC AGE OF CHESS

The period that followed was characterized by the dominance of Italian players, the development of chess theory, and, most significantly, the establishment of international reputations and itinerant champions. Amateur players began to meet and play, forming loosely structured schools and academies. These academies brought

"THE THREE SISTERS PLAYING CHESS," SOFONISBA ANGUISSOLA, ITALIAN (1535–1625), OIL ON CANVAS, 1555

Throughout the medieval period and well into the Renaissance, women played chess in the home with family and close friends. The artist shows us an intimate portrait of herself and her sisters engaged in the game. The set they are playing with is designed as busts on stems and bases, a style that would grow increasingly popular in the 17th, and especially, 18th century.

As sets became more
and more sophisticated,
boards became even more
elaborate and ornamental.
They also became more
practical. Inlaid outside
and inside this box are
boards for chess, *merels*,
or Nine Men's Morris,
and backgammon.
The board shown, *merels*,
was extremely popular
and its origins date back
to 1400 BCE. A variation
of the game, played on
diagonals, is tic-tac-toe.

together some of the best players, and their champions sought out
other players living throughout Europe. This eventually developed a
kind of ad hoc championship play, as a result of which several champions became internationally known. Out of these meetings grew an
interest in intensive analyses of specific games, which were eventually
recorded, printed, and sold throughout Europe.

In many ways the era began with the publication of the *Libro de la
invención liberal y arte de jeugo del axedrez (Book of the Liberal
Invention and Art of Playing Chess)* in 1561 by the Spaniard Ruy
López, a native of Segura. A priest (and later bishop) and chess player
of some note in Spain, López traveled to Italy, where he was introduced into Italian chess-playing circles. Upon his return, he wrote an
extensive analysis of play following the latest innovations. His emphasis on the opening significantly changed the way players approached
the game, making it more aggressive and competitive. After López, a
series of internationally known players rose to stardom, including
Giovanni Leonardo and Paolo Boi, who both achieved an element of
notoriety for their play.

It was the champion Gioachino Greco, however, who brought
advanced play to the rest of Europe. Born in Italy, Greco was largely
uneducated but had an affinity for playing chess. He traveled from
Italy to England in the early 1620s, playing chess with the leading con-
tenders of Europe. Along the way he compiled a collection of chess
problems that he began copying out for patrons and enthusiasts of the
game. His small pamphlets were then transcribed and later printed for

Shâh   Phern   Pil   Asp su Suâr   Ruch

Piyâde   Piyâde   Piyâde   Piyâde   Piyâde   Piyâde

G.S. fecit.

a growing number of chess fans. By 1650 copies of his work could be found throughout Europe. Works by both Greco and López were reprinted well into the eighteenth century, proving their popularity and worth. Other seventeenth-century authors, such as Gustavus Selenus (the pseudonym of Augustus, duke of Brunswick-Lüneburg) and Francis Beale, simply reinterpreted the earlier texts of López and Greco, while adding some of their own ideas.

The renewed interest at this time in the origins and history of chess was simply another expression of intellectual curiosity that the game attracted during this period. In the early seventeenth century, Pietro

Carrera and Alessandro Salvio both published chess books that included histories about the leading players of the day. In fact, much of what is known today about Greco and others are derived from these works.

Other historians delved into the history of the game in a search for answers beyond the fictionalized accounts of the medieval period. In 1694, an English scholar named Thomas Hyde wrote the first comprehensive book about the history of chess, titled *De Ludis Orientalibus.* In the work, Hyde is able to trace the origins of the game back to ancient Persia and India. It is also interesting that Hyde describes both European and Oriental chess pieces. Of course, by that time, chess sets had already become collectors' items as well as playing pieces.

CHESS SETS DURING THE RENAISSANCE

Artisans again picked up their tools to create playing pieces that were reflections of the times. Although it is true that little evidence exists to support the theory that the rapid changes tearing through Europe from the late fifteenth through the seventeenth century affected the stylistic development of chess sets during the period, those sets did clearly change. Whether they were representational or conventional, they expanded upon and even rivaled sets from earlier periods in their materials, subjects, and style. Even so, the many styles and variations produced in Europe were surpassed at times by sets brought back as souvenirs by the military and economic expansionists eager to establish colonial outposts around the world.

PRINTED ILLUSTRATION, THOMAS HYDE, 1694

By the end of the 17th century, chess became the object of serious scholarly research. No longer content to repeat the legends and stories of the past, scholars like Thomas Hyde (1636–1702) began to unravel the history of the game. Hyde, a linguist and interpreter of oriental languages at the English Court, was one of the first European scholars to actually search older Arabic, Persian, and Hebrew texts for references to the game. After exhaustive study, Hyde concluded that chess most likely began in India. This illustration from his book *De Ludis Orientalibus* represents chessmen which the author received from a friend who had brought them back from Bombay, India.

Made more for presentation than for play, representational sets continued to be executed throughout the period. As status symbols, they became increasingly ornate. They could be readily found in fashionable cabinets of curiosities, which displayed a wide range of exquisitely made, unusual, or even bizarre objects that had been collected to reflect the owner's discernment and respectability. In very wealthy households, chess sets might be richly detailed and adorned with precious and semiprecious gems set on pieces made of gold, silver, pewter, or other rich materials. Boards were equally magnificent, made out of gold or silver and often inset with a variety of stones including marble, porphyry, and obsidian. They exemplified some of the finest technical and artistic virtuosity of their day.

Perhaps the most significant change among representational chessmen of the period was that they began to depict a variety of themes. Until the fifteenth century, the dominant representational style tended to be modeled on medieval society. Developments in the arts and sciences, the growth of commerce and the middle class, the rise of nationalism, the beginnings of world exploration, and the study of humanist notions gradually encouraged fine artists to seek out new themes and subjects. Chess makers were no different from their colleagues, and representational sets of the time began to portray subjects derived from everyday life, literature, and history. By the end of the seventeenth century, sets also depicted exotic peoples and represented natural history and science. Clearly, no one theme would ever dominate the subject matter of representational chessmen again.

FIGURES FROM A CHESS SET, GERMAN, IVORY, EBONY, AND SILVER GILT, LATE 16TH CENTURY

Throughout the 16th century, views of foreign lands, strange animals, and unusual plant life provided the inspiration for chess set designs. One side of this set presents Europeans as ancient Romans while the other portrays the native inhabitants of North America. The design of this set may have been inspired by engravings based on watercolors of the New World by the Englishman, John White, and the Frenchman, Jacques Le Moyne de Morgues. Their works were first published in Germany in 1590 and 1591 by the Flemish printer, Theodore de Bry.

In a similar vein, as explorers and state-sponsored envoys established trading outposts and colonies in such exotic places as India, China, and the Americas, they brought back chess sets. From the start, it became popular to collect foreign-made sets, and—like much of the art created for tourists today—the appeal was in the pairing of a known function with an exotic reminder of travel. These sets were either collected from places where chess was played or commissioned from the indigenous artisans. Once their popularity was established, it became common for foreign officials to present chess sets to European dignitaries, princes, or kings.

PLAYING SETS

The rise of a European middle class, eager to emulate the nobility in the late medieval and early Renaissance periods, increased the demand for luxury items such as chess sets. However, only the wealthiest of them could afford the labor-intensive representational sets. The majority of the middle class sought out less expensive ones. Likewise, serious players not only wanted inexpensive sets, but ones that were better suited to the new game that was becoming widely popular. Representational sets tended to be cumbersome in play and too fragile for travel; players wanted sets that were functional, simple, and easily transportable.

To meet the demand, artisans turned once again to the lathe. A workhorse since ancient times, the lathe could rapidly and inexpen-

"THE GAME OF CHESS," LUCAS VAN LEYDEN, DUTCH, (1494-1533), OIL ON PANEL, 1508

The board shown has ninety-six squares (12 x 8) and possibly depicts a variation of chess known as the "Courier's Game." In this variant, the players have the usual number of chessmen plus two couriers, a counselor, and four more pawns. The game was established by the 13th century and played until at least the 17th century when it must have fallen into disuse. Variants of chess were extremely popular throughout the Medieval period, and well into the 15th and 16th centuries. Europeans, with an eye to speeding up the game, experimented with them. Ultimately it was a variant from the south of Europe, first known as the "Queen's Chess" that became the modern game of chess. The pieces depicted in this painting show conventional playing pieces of the early 16th century.

CHESSBOARD AND SET, ITALY, HORN, BONE, AND WOOD, C. 1450

This extraordinary Florentine board and conventional chessmen were made by the Italian master carver and turner, Baldassarre Embriachi. Turned on a lathe, the pieces are one of the few surviving examples of conventionally designed chessmen of the period. Embriachi's rook, flowering outwardly to either side, is an elegant refinement of rook types unearthed from excavations at Novgorod, Russia, dating from the 12th century. The style and shape of these older cousins, suggest that the ancestor of Embriachi's rook may very well be the abstracted shape of the Arab chariot piece.

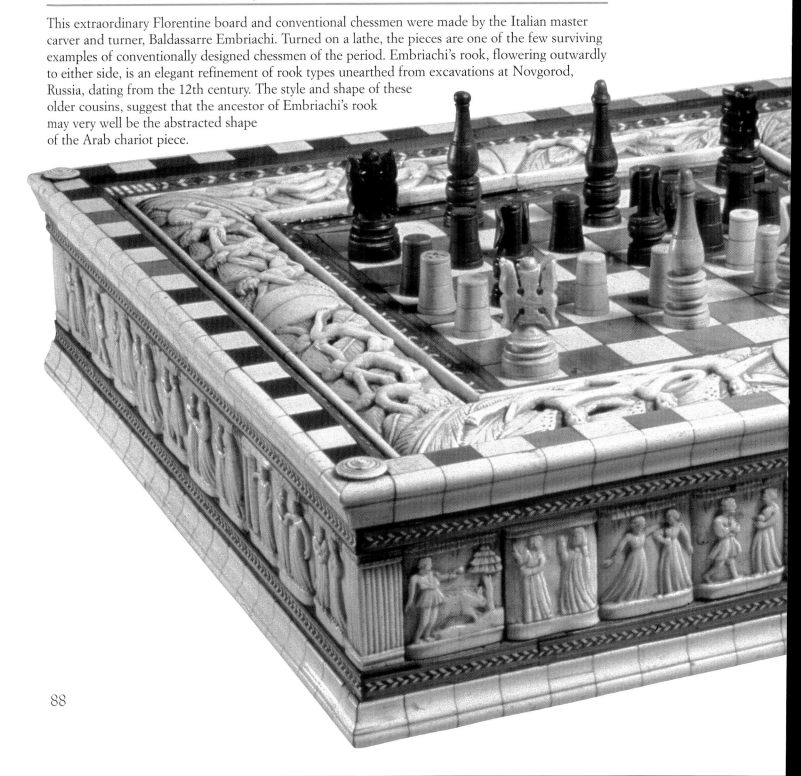

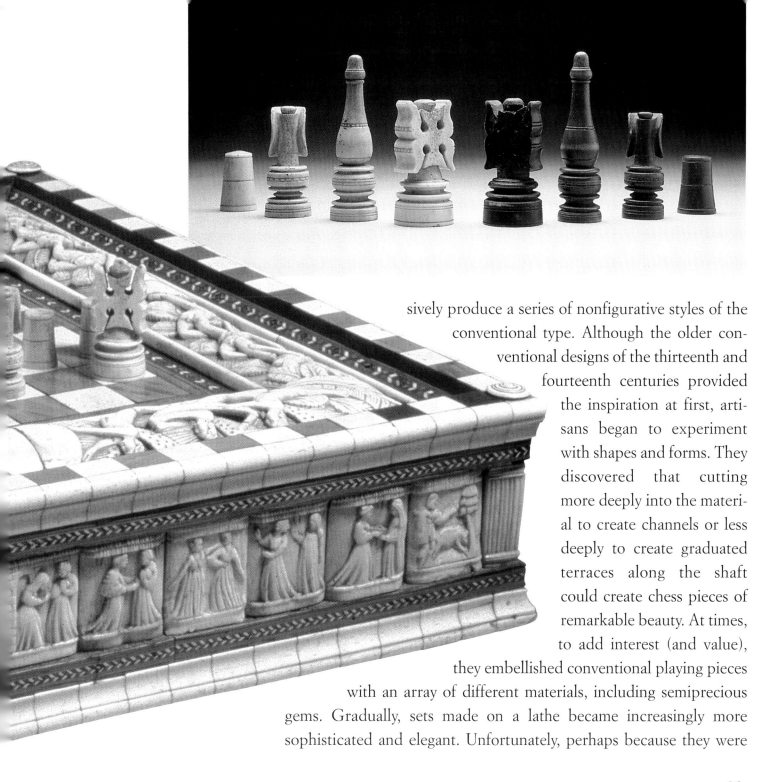

sively produce a series of nonfigurative styles of the conventional type. Although the older conventional designs of the thirteenth and fourteenth centuries provided the inspiration at first, artisans began to experiment with shapes and forms. They discovered that cutting more deeply into the material to create channels or less deeply to create graduated terraces along the shaft could create chess pieces of remarkable beauty. At times, to add interest (and value), they embellished conventional playing pieces with an array of different materials, including semiprecious gems. Gradually, sets made on a lathe became increasingly more sophisticated and elegant. Unfortunately, perhaps because they were

Printed illustration, German, 1616

The author of *Das Schach oder König-Spiel* (Chess or the King Game), is shown staring inquisitively toward the viewer. Augustus, Duke of Brunswick-Lüneburg (1579–1666) took the pseudonym of Gustavus Selenus, and published this book in 1616. Although the work was largely based on an earlier work by the Spanish priest and chess champion, Ruy López, Selenus added some interesting historical information and, more importantly, illustrated his book with drawings depicting a style of chessmen that had developed in central Europe and Germany. Consequently, the style became known as the Selenus style.

designed for play rather than display, few of these playing pieces have survived. They are largely known today because they were extensively illustrated in paintings, engravings, and documentary material from the period. Indeed, by the number of illustrations found, it seems that, as in earlier periods, conventional sets were much more common than their survival would indicate.

Although lathe-turned sets could be made of almost any medium, hardwood was frequently the material of choice. It was inexpensively priced, was well suited to being shaped on the lathe, and could easily be painted or gilded when finished to give it a rich appearance. An ideal alternative to expensive ivory was bone, though it was somewhat more labor-intensive than wood. Before work could begin, fats and fibrous matter left on the bone had to be removed and then the bone had to be kiln-dried. The resulting hard material was no problem for a lathe. As lathe technology developed and steel bits were introduced, conventional chess pieces were even made from stone such as jade, obsidian, and porphyry.

Although increasingly elegant in form and shape, conventionally designed sets were, at times, too abstract. Distinguishing one piece from another during a game was often difficult for a player, particularly when an unfamiliar set was used. As international play increased, and reputations were at stake, it quickly became apparent that there was a need to more easily differentiate between the pieces.

Perhaps the most sophisticated expression of a conventionally turned set of this type was what became known as the Selenus style,

Overleaf:

SELENUS STYLE
CHESS SETS, EARLY AND
MID-19TH CENTURY,
BONE

INLAID FRUITWOOD
BOARD, 17TH CENTURY,
CENTRAL EUROPE
OR GERMANY

Selenus-style chessmen have been manufactured from the 15th until the turn of the 19th century. Typically they are made in sections on a lathe, then chased and screwed together. They were quite often made of wood or bone, but finer sets were made from ivory. In the 19th century, German master turners established their credentials by producing a chess set based on the Selenus style. One such master, Michael Edel, set a standard of craftsmanship emulated throughout Germany. His sets are typically characterized by the rook, which he presented as a church bell tower. The set pictured on the right and in the inset above, was designed after an Edel model. The fruitwood board combines a backgammon board on the inside and a chessboard on the outside.

CALVERT-STYLE CHESS SET, GREAT BRITAIN, IVORY, MID-19TH CENTURY

Chess set designs based on the Selenus style made by German turners in the mid-19th century may have influenced master turners in London to produce variations of the style with a distinctly British flavor. Besides favoring a slightly stockier appearance, British turners preferred the English-styled bishop over those employed by their colleagues on the continent. The so-called Calvert style, with its characteristic petalled tops, was manufactured by a number of houses including Lund and Jaques of London.

after drawings in Gustavus Selenus's 1616 book on chess, *Das Schach oder König-Spiel* (Chess or the King Game). Essentially the work of Ruy López from decades earlier, Selenus's book added printed images of chess sets. These sets, with their elegant lathe-turned bases and shafts, were embellished with tiers upon which rested cut circlets resembling crowns. The pieces were distinguished from one another by height, the number of tiers, and sometimes symbols atop the pieces. Such was the popularity of this style that it continued to be made well into the nineteenth century.

Over time, other attempts were made to design plain pieces distinguishable from each other. Although the ultimate solution would have to wait until the creation of the Staunton set in the mid-nineteenth century, makers of chess sets gradually accepted certain design criteria. It became commonly understood that the king and queen were the tallest pieces and often had a symbolic reference to a crown of some kind. The bishop, knight, and rook were generally similar in height to one another and distinguished by different symbols on abstracted shafts. An assortment of symbols evolved: the knight was represented by a horse's head, the bishop by an abstracted miter, the rook by a tower, and the smaller pawn by a simple knob. Combining the schematic nonrepresentational design with a symbol representing each distinct piece created a uniquely European set, which anticipated the modern playing pieces of the nineteenth century.

CHAPTER SIX
CHESS IN THE INDUSTRIAL AGE

"Chess was intended to be the recreation of men of genius and practical energies. . . who even in their amusements, are desirous of bracing and invigorating to the utmost their intellectual powers."

— HOWARD STAUNTON

B Y THE BEGINNING OF the eighteenth century, more people than ever were finding that they had time on their hands, and they were filling it with an endless variety of leisure activities. These included not only theaters but museums, libraries, large urban festivals, and amusement parks. Games of all sorts, particularly ones involving gambling, became favorite pastimes. The popularity of card games in particular could have seriously challenged chess had it not been for a growing interest in competitive play. Over the course of the next two hundred years the relatively modest groups of players that existed by the end of the seventeenth century would grow in numbers, eventually drawing members from all levels of society. In the process, chess became

CHESS SET AND BOARD, FRENCH, DIEPPE STYLE IVORY AND RUSSIAN LEATHER, LATE 18TH CENTURY

Napoleon was fond of chess, often stopping in at the famous Café de la Régence, to play or watch games in progress. Oddly, one of his playing sets, shown here, represented the French monarchy on one side and the Africans on the other. The irony of this was not lost on Napoleon who was reported to once remark after his king accidently fell to the floor, "Oh my poor Louis XVIII, there you are ruined."

**CHESS SET,
RUSSIAN,
CONVENTIONAL
STYLE,
STEEL AND BRONZE
WITH GOLD AND
SILVER INLAY,
1782**

This set was made for
Catherine the Great by a
craftsman from the Royal
Armory in Tula named
Adrian Sukhanova.
The set arrived in a steel
casket with eighty pieces
(five half sets) as a not so
subtle reminder that the
Czarina had promised to
build a new Royal Armory.
Although she never
fulfilled her promise,
Catherine the Great
was fond of chess and
undoubtedly appreciated
the gift.

egalitarian. The roots of this amazing transition took place in the early decades of the eighteenth century in northern Europe.

Although Italy and Spain had dominated play in Europe in the first decades of the seventeenth century, by the beginning of the eighteenth century there was a significant shift in chess activity toward the North. Chess already had a tradition in the courts of France and England. The sixteenth-century queens Catherine de Medici of France and Elizabeth I of England were both known to keenly enjoy the game, as did many of the politicians, historians, scientists, poets, and other hangers-on at court. The reputation that these courts acquired attracted some of the best players of Europe well into the second half of the eighteenth century. (The Hague, in the Netherlands, was the home from 1710 to 1730 of one of the most notable champions of the period, the famous Scots player Alexander Cunningham.) It was in the charged atmospheres of the English and French courts that the American envoy Benjamin Franklin astounded everyone with his passion for the game.

Outside the royal courts, loose confederacies of players began to gather in the ever-present coffeehouses that sprang up throughout Europe at the end of the seventeenth century. These establishments attracted some of the best minds of Europe as they became forums where the latest news and ideas were exchanged. It was not uncommon for like-minded individuals to congregate at the same coffeehouse, and some establishments quickly became associated with certain intellectual pursuits. Because chess was now thoroughly linked to intellec-

tual activity, it was inevitable that the coffeehouses attracted players. There, amateurs and champions alike could meet, mix, play, and exchange ideas. By 1730, it was clear that some of the most exciting play in Europe was to be found in Paris and London.

In France, the best players could be found at the Café de la Régence, at the Palais Royal in Paris. Established sometime during the second decade of the eighteenth century, the Café de la Régence quickly developed a reputation as a leading center for chess in France. In England, Slaughter's Coffee House on St. Martin's Lane drew the

CHESS SET, FRENCH, IVORY, C. 1750

This very charming and elegant animal set is thought to have been made in either Lyon or Paris, and demonstrates the enormous skill of 18th-century French ivory carvers. It depicts a lion and lioness as the king and queen, stags as bishops, horses as knights, and dogs as pawns. The hounds are particularly touching as each exhibits a personality of its own.

chess buffs of London. Until the French Revolution, close links existed between these two informal centers of chess. Matches took place at both, and champions traveled back and forth between Paris and London. The play, discussions about the games, and resulting publications produced by the diverse groups of people drawn to these coffeehouses dramatically altered the history of the game and set the stage for the modern era of chess. The period was dominated by French players, and two of the most prominent of them began their careers in the coffeehouses of Paris. They were Philip Stamma and André Philidor.

STAMMA AND PHILIDOR

Little is known about the Syrian-born Philip Stamma until his appearance in Paris sometime in the 1730s, where he soon became known as an accomplished player. In 1737 he wrote his *Essai sur le Jeu des Échecs,* which brought him to the attention of the English. Under the patronage of Lord Harrington, he relocated to London, where in 1745 he published an English edition of his book, *The Noble Game of Chess.* Although Stamma claimed that the chess problems in his book were derived from Arabic sources, in reality they were largely his own. Despite the cover story the real significance of Stamma's work was twofold. Not only was his book the first in nearly two hundred years to present a collection of chess problems, but it also challenged prevailing notions about chess that were largely based on

102

the work of Gioachino Greco first published a century earlier. Stamma's work opened the door to a new age of chess analysis, and its importance was such that it continued to be published until the beginning of the nineteenth century.

It was, however, the Frenchman François-André Danican Philidor (1726–1795) who was to become the reigning player of the century. Younger than Stamma, Philidor was a musician of some repute before he became a chess champion. His skill in chess awed and amazed his contemporaries, immortalizing him even in his own time. Like Stamma, Philidor traveled between Paris and London playing and demonstrating chess, including such feats as blindfolded chess and multiple games at the same time. Even though his remarkable abilities would have energized the development of chess in France and England alone, Philidor's most significant contribution to the game was a book he wrote in 1749, *Analyse du jeu des échecs*. In it, Philidor created a series of nine games in which he placed a great deal of emphasis on the play of the pawns. His book was written for people who knew the basics of the game and wanted to learn more. It

François-André Danican Philidor (1726–1795), the famed French champion, often engaged in blindfolded competitions such as this one at the British club, Parsloe. The event, written up in *Sporting Magazine* in 1794, was considered an amazing accomplishment on the part of Philidor.

PLAYING SET, BRITISH, IVORY, LATE 18TH/EARLY 19TH CENTURIES

This set, once owned by Lord Nelson and subsequently acquired by a friend and shipmate, Captain Seymour of the British Royal Navy, is a typical British playing set of the period. The set was stained green on one side and left white on the other.

On his European tour of 1858, Paul Morphy (1837–1884), the first American world
champion, demonstrated his extraordinary abilities by playing eight opponents
simultaneously at the Café de la Régence in Paris. He won six and drew two.
The event astonished Americans at home, and brought Morphy coverage in *Harper's
Weekly*, where this engraving appeared. Like Bobby Fischer, Morphy rocketed to
stardom, and then at the height of his powers, quit playing chess altogether.

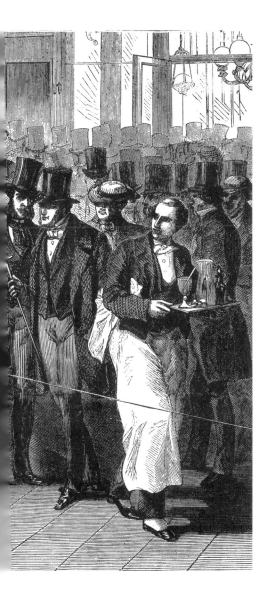

became widely popular and was published in several languages well into the nineteenth century. In 1750 the book was issued in English under the title *Chess Analyzed*, and in 1754 it came out in German under the title *Die Kunst im Schachspiel ein Meister zu werden*.

By the beginning of the nineteenth century, players like Stamma, Philidor, and all the others from the Café de la Régence and Slaughter's helped to establish Paris and London as the leading centers of the chess world. Supported by patrons, these men laid the groundwork for a rudimentary support structure for chess that became the starting point for further developments in the next century. Because of this, chess in the nineteenth century would expand to encompass the rise of clubs as well as international and tournament play, dramatically transforming chess into an organized sport.

THE RISE OF CHESS CLUBS

A natural outgrowth of the coffeehouses was the development of chess clubs, which sprang up in urban centers throughout Europe and the United States in the first decades of the nineteenth century. It did not matter that they tended to form and disband rather rapidly at first (the noted exception being the London Chess Club, established in 1807). They nonetheless encouraged a codification of chess rules, developed and sponsored championship matches, and encouraged the printing of books and pamphlets. These clubs provided the means for chess to became self-supporting, organized,

The dapper Howard Staunton, seen here in a c. 1840 photograph, was, in his mind's eye, first a Shakespearean scholar and then a chess player. But in the eyes of the world, and especially the British public, he was a world-champion chess player.

and more urbane. Their appeal to individuals of diverse backgrounds resulted in a larger constituency and support system. Chess would no longer have to rely on the vagaries of patronage; it could rely on itself.

Significantly, as the clubs grew in size, they began to sponsor tournaments. They found backers, advertised, and operated tournaments, keeping the players out of the business side of the game. An important by-product of all of this was that championship play was streamlined, standardized, and made accessible to all players. The establishment of a point system and time limits (resulting in the development of the chess clock) helped to regulate larger tournaments, making them easier to manage. For the first time in its history, chess was an organized sport, and as matches and prizes increased, it became possible to make an independent living as a chess player.

One of the most famous champions of the day was also its strongest promoter. A man of enormous ego and dramatic presence, Howard Staunton (1810–1874) almost single-handedly wrested from the French their superior position, making London the capital of the chess world in the second half of the nineteenth century. His skill was matched only by his ability to promote the game, and throughout his career he worked like a demon on its behalf, lending his name to a variety of chess causes. From 1845 until his death in 1874, Staunton wrote a chess column for the *Illustrated London News*, in which he staunchly supported chess but also maddeningly critiqued colleagues, matches, and clubs. The ensuing controversies served to infuse the game with new energy and excitement. All in all, Staunton did more for the development of the game than any other chess player in its history.

The excitement that Staunton and other Englishmen generated was infectious, bringing players from all over Europe and the United States to London. One of these was the American Paul Morphy (1837–1884). Chess had been played in the United States since before the movement for independence from Great Britain. A number of important early American political figures played chess, including George Washington, Benjamin Franklin, and Thomas Jefferson (Franklin had been so intrigued by the game that in 1779 he wrote a pamphlet, *The Morals of Chess)*. Morphy had already proved his great skill at home before being drawn to Europe to try his hand with some of Europe's best, especially Staunton. Although he never met Staunton in a match, Morphy did have a triumphal tour of Europe in 1858, winning his matches easily and with apparent genius. Shortly thereafter, however, he returned home and lost interest in championship play.

Throughout the nineteenth century, as purses became larger, competition became fiercer. Although the newly emerging chess organizations tightened rules and standardized play, perhaps the most significant outcome of these highly competitive matches was that they attracted the interest of the general public. Champions such as Morphy or Staunton strongly appealed to national pride, but there was also a general revival of an interest in the game itself. After all, chess might be played anywhere by anyone with the ability to reason and think logically. Chess sets appeared in homes either on their own or packaged in collections with other popular middle-class games. Indeed, lovers of the game could even take their passion with them in sets specifically designed for travel. These trends would bloom and thrive in the twentieth century, when chess would enter the political arena as part of the wrangling between the West and the Soviet Union, and also flourish in hundreds of thousands of local chess clubs that would form around the world.

CHESS SETS IN THE INDUSTRIAL AGE

Facing page, bottom:

JOHN JAQUES WHITTINGTON TRAVEL SET, GREAT BRITAIN, BONE AND WOOD, C. 1890–1920

Special traveling sets were used to help pass the time on long tedious train trips. With pieces that pegged into holes drilled into the board, these ingenious sets could be easily folded up mid-game, locking the playing pieces in place so that the players might continue the game elsewhere. Similar sets were made in the United States until the 1940s.

Over the centuries, representational sets have always been popular. Starting in the eighteenth century, however, the variety of themes and subject matter that were represented rose to new heights. European expansion and the exploration of new worlds, geographically and scientifically, brought a wealth of new ideas and themes to be exploited. Highbrow themes warred with the sentimental, cute, and mundane. Inspiration came from popular literature, folktales, historical sources, and even current events. Each design, subject, and theme that was used encouraged the next generation and the one after that. Representational sets were greatly admired for their workmanship and beauty and were often collected for display. In general, they were made to impress, and they generally did. As the eighteenth and then the nineteenth centuries advanced, sets were

GAMES COMPENDIA, GREAT BRITAIN, WOOD, BONE, PAPER, 19TH CENTURY

Beautifully made game sets like this one (top right) housed a wide variety of games including chess, backgammon, checkers, dice, dominos, cribbage, bizet, cards, and in this case, a horse-racing game. Games Compendia, as they were called, contained games from a variety of toy and game manufacturers in Britain. Featured in this compendia is a Staunton-style chess set that conveniently sits on pegs in the box when the set is not in use.

PAWNS, ROOK, AND KING, SWITZERLAND, BEARS OF BERNE, FRUITWOOD, 19TH CENTURY

Wood carvers from Switzerland are famous the world over for beautiful carvings made out of fruit- and hardwoods. Although sets have been made with a variety of themes, one of the more enduring has been this one known as the Bears of Berne. These sets comprise bears engaged in various human activities. The center for this type of carving was near Brienz Lake in the Bernese Alps, a popular tourist destination since the 19th century.

created from new materials made possible by the technologies of the industrial age. Still, traditional materials such as bone, wood, and ivory remained popular into the twentieth century. Ivory was particularly coveted and some of the most elegant sets of the period were made of this luxurious material. Ivory workshops throughout Europe produced an abundant number of sets in a range of styles and themes.

As a result of the increase in popularity of the material during the course of the seventeenth century, ivory manufacturing centers soon developed. Some of the busiest took root in the cities of London and Birmingham in England, Dieppe and Paris in France, and Kholmogory in Russia. Both Dieppe and Kholmogory became so closely associated with the type of sets manufactured in the workshops of those cities that each lent its name to a particular style. Although striking presentation sets were designed and made from virgin ivory, most sets were fashioned from the leftover scraps of larger projects. The pieces were either hand-carved or turned on a lathe

COUNSELOR OR VIZIER (QUEEN), RUSSIA, KHOLMOGORY STYLE, WALRUS IVORY, 17TH–18TH CENTURY

Ivory workshops in and around Kholmogory, Russia, have been producing walrus and fossilized ivory sets since the seventeenth century. This type, the so-called Kholmogory style, typically pits Russians against Orientals. Interestingly, the Russian pawns are represented by Roman soldiers. It has been suggested that this is a reflection of Catherine the Great's personal bodyguard, whom she had dressed in this manner. The use of a counselor or vizier instead of the Western queen suggests that chess in Russia maintained some Eastern attributes long after they had disappeared in the West.

CHESS SET, FRENCH, DIEPPE STYLE, IVORY, 18TH CENTURY

When chess was first adopted by the French, the craftsmen of the day interpreted the elephant piece of the Arabs as a *fou* or fool. Other Europeans preferred to interpret the piece as a bishop. Both of the 18th-century Dieppe sets on this page have fools instead of bishops.

CHESS SET, FRENCH, DIEPPE STYLE, IVORY, C. 1750

The ivory-carving industry of Dieppe dates back to the beginning of the French trade with West Africa. Ivory carvers, living and working in this French port on the English Channel, specialized in sets like these to such an extent that they have become known as the Dieppe style. Characterized by busts on stems and bases, these sets often represent the opposing sides of the French colonial and African forces in Morocco, Zanzibar, Senegal, or the French Cameroon.

or made with a combination of these techniques. Even though African ivory was preferred because of its hardness and easy accessibility, Indian ivory was also used. A few workshops, most notably the Russian workshops at Kholmogory, used walrus and fossilized mastodon ivories. For the most part, however, ivory was expensive and labor-intensive, and therefore did not lend itself well to the increasing but not so affluent market for representational chess sets.

A rising demand for less expensive sets, and advances in technology, made possible the diverse range of themes and subject matter in sets. Hard-paste porcelain, developed by the German ceramist Johann Friedrich Böttger in 1708, was an ideal material from which to manufacture chess sets. Porcelain was popular during the period and was often prominently displayed in the home. Many of the noted porcelain houses of the eighteenth century, including Limoges and Sèvres of France, Wedgwood of Britain, and Meissen of Germany, produced chess sets, largely as curio pieces. The sets made in these workshops

FAIENCE SET AND BOARD, FRENCH, RÉGENCE STYLE, CERAMIC, 19TH–20TH CENTURY

Faience sets of the Régence style have been made in France since the early 19th century in the ceramic and porcelain centers of Rouen, Gien, and Paris. Faience is a fine tin-glazed earthenware capable of receiving brilliant enamels such as the blue, green, yellow, and red seen in this set.

114

CHESS SET AND BOARD, GERMAN, SEA LIFE SET AND BOARD, MEISSEN PORCELAIN FACTORY, PORCELAIN, 1926-1928

The Meissen Porcelain Factory has been producing fine porcelain since 1710, and chess sets since the mid-1750s. In the 1920s, Meissen began producing sets designed by sculptor-trained Max Easer (1885–1945). This captivating set presents the underwater world of the ocean. The knights are seahorses, the bishops are octopuses, rooks are lobsters, and the king and queen appear to be different-sized corals. The pawns are represented by starfish. All of these watery creatures reside on a board which undulates in curvilinear wave patterns around the outside rim.

were small, elegant, and at times whimsical and sentimental. Although a few conventional-style sets were made in porcelain, most were representational.

The manufacture of porcelain chess sets in the eighteenth century only hinted at the possibilities of mass-produced chess sets brought on by the industrial revolution of the nineteenth century. Even though sets made out of precious metals had been created for hundreds of years, modern technology allowed manufacturers to produce metal sets inexpensively, opening up new markets among the middle and lower classes. Among the more notable are

CHESS SET, GERMANY, ZIMMERMAN STYLE, CAST IRON, C. 1850–1875

Starting in the 19th century, a number of German manufacturers began to produce cast-iron chessmen like these. The most famous, E. G. Zimmerman of Hanau near Frankfurt, lent his name to the style. Cast-iron sets are generally characterized by accurate and finely articulated details. This set may represent the Muslims against the Crusaders.

the small cast silver, pewter, and even iron sets produced by German and other central European manufacturers. As beautiful and charming as these representational sets were, however, it was the conventional or playing sets that were to see the most dramatic changes over the course of the eighteenth and nineteenth centuries.

CONVENTIONAL SETS AND THE STAUNTON STYLE

The increased interest in the game, particularly in international play during the late eighteenth and early nineteenth centuries, brought about a renewed demand for a more universal model for chess pieces. The variety and styles of the conventional form begun in the fifteenth century had expanded tremendously by the beginning of the nineteenth century. Some of the more common conventional types popular during the period included the English Barleycorn, the St. George, the French Régence (named after the Café de la Régence in Paris), and the central European Selenus styles. Most pieces were tall, easily tipped, and cumbersome during play. But their largest sin was the uniformity of the pieces within a set. A player's unfamiliarity with an opponent's set could tragically alter the outcome of a game. By the early decades of the nineteenth century, it was all too clear that there was a great need for a playing set with pieces that were easy to use and universally recognized by players of diverse backgrounds. The solution, first released in 1849 by the purveyors of fine games, John Jaques of London, was to become known as the Staunton chess set after the English and world champion, Howard Staunton.

CHESS SET, FRENCH, RÉGENCE STYLE, BONE, 19TH CENTURY

This French conventional style was a favorite playing set from the mid-18th century well into the 20th. It was named after the Café de la Régence in the Palais Royal where all of France's noted chess players and intellectuals gathered to play and talk about chess. Benjamin Franklin, in Paris representing the American government, also frequented the establishment, and owned a set in the Régence style.

BARLEYCORN SETS, GREAT BRITAIN, BONE, 19TH CENTURY

Barleycorn sets, so-called because of the leaf motif encircling the main shaft of the kings and queens of some sets, were widely used by players throughout 19th-century Britain. The style was a favorite across the Atlantic as well. George Washington and Thomas Jefferson both owned fine examples. Barleycorn chessmen were made in sections on a lathe, then chased and screwed together. Although they were generally made of inexpensive bone, it is not uncommon to find a set made of ivory. Prior to the outbreak of hostilities during the Napoleonic War, Britain had been in the habit of importing fine ivory and bone sets from Dieppe. When the war put a halt to this, British turners increased the quality and production of chess sets, and the industry quickly developed a reputation for fine playing sets.

Although Nathaniel Cook has long been credited with the design, more than likely it was conceived by his brother-in-law and owner of the firm, John Jaques. Jaques, a master turner, had probably been experimenting with a design that would not only be accepted by players but could also be produced at a reasonable cost. In the end, he most likely borrowed and synthesized elements from sets already available to create a design of sheer brilliance. The key was the use of universally recognizable symbols atop conventional stems and bases. Moreover, the pieces were compact, well balanced, and weighted to provide a playing set that was as useful as it was understandable.

MODERN CLUB-SIZED STAUNTON CHESS SET, BOXWOOD AND EBONY, AMERICAN, 1998 AND ORIGINAL CARTON-PIERRE CASE, BRITISH, COMPOSITION, 1855

For over a century and a half, this style has been cherished by players around the world. The first Staunton sets were registered on March 1, 1849, and were available to the general public by September of the same year. The superiority of the design lay in its well-balanced, easily recognized pieces. Such was its success that it is still the style of choice for play to this day. Jaques originally sold the sets in handsome composition boxes, called carton-pierre cases, like the one here. Pictured with it are modern Staunton chessmen based on designs made by John Jaques between 1849 and 1852 and currently being produced by an American company, The House of Staunton.

Jaques then approached his brother-in-law for advice. Cook registered the set with the Patent Office in 1849, and as Howard Staunton's editor, convinced the champion to endorse the set. Staunton not only endorsed the product for Jaques of London but promoted it to an extraordinary degree in the *Illustrated London News*—including the lambasting and derision of any other design of chessmen then proposed. The Staunton style, as it became known, was soon the standard on which most tournament playing pieces have been made and used around the globe ever since.

Left:
The original 1849 drawing picturing both the chess set and the carton-pierre case that Nathaniel Cook used to apply for the patent.

Below:
The inspiration for the Staunton knight can be found in the reliefs (447–432 BCE) from the north frieze of the Parthenon now housed in the British Museum. The Elgin Marbles were named after Lord Elgin, the man responsible for bringing the frieze to England in 1806. They became an instant success with the British public and were eventually sold to the British government in 1916. As a youth, John Jaques would have been caught up in the frenzy surrounding the Elgin Marbles. Later, when he was looking for something on which to base the design of his knight, it must have seemed the ideal model.

123

Right:

CHESS SET, BRITISH, ROSE CHESSMEN, CAST LEAD WITH RED AND BLACK LACQUER 1942

The Rose Chessmen, named after Mildred Rose who patented it, is a World War II–era set modeled after the Staunton playing pieces. The popularity of the original Staunton design inspired countless variations from the moment it was marketed down to the present day. The adoption of the Staunton design by the World Chess Federation in 1924 as the official style for tournament play served to encourage variants of the style. Literally hundreds exist today.

Left:

CHESS SET, ANGLO-CHINESE, IVORY, LATE 19TH CENTURY

The Staunton style was emulated everywhere, including Asia. This set, based on the Staunton design, charms with interwoven patterns of foliage, birds, and insects across its surface. It was created expressly for the trade, and imported by the British from Canton.

COLLECTING CHESS SETS

The trend toward collecting chess sets began with the cabinets of curiosities of earlier periods and slowly grew throughout the eighteenth and nineteenth centuries. Although it never reached the obsessive stage characteristic of the twentieth century, it was not uncommon for a middle-class household to display at least one fine set, and some homes might have several. Probably the largest enticement to collecting chess sets during this period was the growing availability of chessmen made elsewhere. The tenuous trade contacts of the sixteenth and seventeenth centuries were by now fully established, and the French, Dutch, Spanish, Portuguese, and English had founded colonies throughout the world. Many items brought back from these faraway lands excited comment and interest. Perhaps because they effectively juxtaposed the everyday with the exotic, foreign-made sets may have been particularly appealing.

At the same time, native players in India, China, and much of the rest of Asia played variations of chess that had developed since its beginnings in the fifth or sixth century. Chinese chess had spread to the northeastern edge of the Asian continent before crossing the water to Japan. The Arab form of the game dominated play in India, as it had ever since Muslims had politically subjugated the country centuries earlier. From there it had spread eastward along the southern edge of the continent into parts of Southeast Asia. Everywhere that the Europeans and later the Americans established colonies or

**PAWN AND KNIGHT,
CHINESE,
IVORY,
19TH CENTURY**

A mounted knight and a pawn from an ivory set created for the export market. It was probably imported from Canton, a British trading port since the eighteenth century.

Below:

CHESS SET, CHINESE, IVORY, 19TH CENTURY

With an eye toward the interests of the European buyers, Chinese artisans carved bust figures representing European monarchs on one side of a set and oriental rulers on the other. The style depicted here, with busts on pedestals, is yet another variation on this theme designed by Canton carvers for the Western market.

trading outposts in this corner of the world, they found chess.

The small number of Eastern sets that made it back to Europe must have been considered novelties. In general, the Western market demanded foreign-made sets in the Western tradition. Therefore, chess sets imported from trading centers in the East, and later from regions in Africa and the Arctic, were modeled on the Western version of the game and designed to appeal to Western tastes. Quite often they were also manufactured to Western specifications. In some cases, European-styles were emulated; however, these sets often exhibited the unique cultural characteristics of their origins. Although the

Above:

CHESS SET, CHINESE, IVORY, 19TH CENTURY

By the end of the 18th century, the British East India Company had established trade with China. Back at home, Europeans were profoundly interested in anything Chinese, and by the beginning of the 19th century, Chinese imports of all kinds were in demand, including chess sets. In response to the particularities of the European market, Chinese artists began carving sets with European monarchs on the white side opposing Chinese emperors on the other. This set may represent King George III and his wife, Charlotte, who reigned in Great Britain from 1760 until 1820.

PUZZLE-BALL CHESS SET, CHINESE, IVORY, 19TH CENTURY

Because of their technical virtuoso, puzzle-ball sets are perhaps among the most impressive chessmen to come out of China. Figures representing the Chinese court sit on top of a series of nested balls carved from a solid piece of ivory. Working from the outside, the carver gradually releases each ball, one inside the other, from the ivory. Large sets like this can have up to seven or more concentric balls nested within one another.

overleaf:

CHESS SET, CHINESE, IVORY, C. 1960

Even as late as the latter half of the 20th century, Chinese artisans continued to produce chessmen of exceptional distinction and quality. Contemporary sets sometimes represent historical periods in Chinese history. The dark side of this set may depict the Qing (Ch'ing) dynasty (1644–1912) while the white side may represent the Ming dynasty (1368–1644).

131

This set may represent the conflict between the French and English troops at Pondicherry, where the French lost a decisive battle for control of India to the British in 1761. Several skirmishes followed over the next several decades, and control of the Pondicherry region alternated between the French and English. However, by 1814, the French had once again gained the upper hand. They finally released control of Pondicherry in 1954 to the government of India. Although the turmoil between the French and the British at Pondicherry existed long before the French Revolution of 1789, the vizier (queen) on the French side looks suspiciously like the Emperor Napoleon. Sets like these were coveted, and singular examples were often presented to dignitaries or heads of state.

appeal of these sets initially may have lain in their exotic flavor, they were also admired for their skillful craftsmanship, elaborate detail, and embellishment, as well as for the rich materials from which they were made.

The English established trade relations with India as early as 1600, during the reign of Queen Elizabeth I. By the mid-eighteenth century, the British East India Company's trade interests in the region extended to chess sets, which they began exporting for sale in Europe. Early Indian-made sets quite often depicted the British forces in opposition to either other European nations (usually the French) or local rulers for control of India. They were characterized by the depiction of elephants with howdahs on their backs, as well as camels, horses, and infantry equipped with all the necessary accoutrements for battle. One of the more famous types, the so-called John Company style, acquired its sobriquet in reference to all the sunburned young Englishmen, called "Johns" by the locals, who were employed by the British East India Company. Another favorite, once called Madras, but now more commonly called the Rajasthan, is distinguished by large pieces of ivory, painted or dyed bright red and green.

Besides representational sets such as these, Indian artisans created several of the conventional types. Using European models, most notably the Barleycorn and Staunton, they turned out beautiful lathe-made sets intricately embellished with fine crisscrossing, curvilinear lines of tracery. Oddly enough, the popularity of Indian-made conventional sets resulted in a small market of European-made knockoffs for sale to Westerners interested in acquiring exotic items.

In the Far East, European interests were first established by the Portuguese in Macao in 1557. Shortly thereafter, Spain and Holland established trading ports along the Chinese coastline, and finally the English entered Canton during the seventeenth century. Over the next three hundred years, relations between European powers and China ranged from congenial and uneasy to intense and confrontational. Initially, trade items from the Far East trickled into Europe, surprising Europeans with their beauty and exotic nature. By the end of the eighteenth century, Chinese art, porcelain, and other types of objects were highly prized in Europe, collected, and treasured by the well-to-do and those wanting to emulate them. The resulting fashion for anything Chinese probably encouraged the trade in chess sets made in the Orient. Thus, by the end of the eighteenth century, Chinese

overleaf:
CHESS SET, INDIA, RAJASTHAN STYLE, PAINTED IVORY, LATE 18TH CENTURY

Variations in this style, characterized by howdahs on the backs of elephants, have existed for centuries. The chess scholar Thomas Hyde illustrated such a set in his book on chess in 1694, and a similar set in the Staatliche Kunstsammlungen Historisches Museum in Dresden has an irrefutable date of 1610. The British forces, easily recognized by pawns wearing the distinctive red coats and military hat of the Hussars, carry fixed bayonets. In this set the British pawn like the one at right, carries and plays a fife. They confront the Indian forces represented by pawns wearing traditional Indian dress carrying spears and longbows.

137

138

139

CHESS SET, INDIA, SAHIB STYLE, IVORY, 19TH CENTURY

Chessmen designed as busts on pedestal bases were carved in India for trade from the late 19th into the early 20th century. A favorite theme was the religious and political conflict between the Sikhs and Muslims. The so-called Sahib sets, like this one, present this long-standing animosity between the two groups. This set was probably made in Delhi.

craftspeople began to fashion sets made exclusively for European markets. One of the earliest themes presented elaborately detailed Chinese figures in theatrical dress. Later sets, known as puzzle-balls, displayed Chinese figures on top of an intricately carved ball housing five to seven balls, one within the other. By the nineteenth century, Chinese artists were carving sets that represented the Chinese on one side and specific European rulers—such as Napoleon and King George III—on the other, deliberately appealing to the taste of the European buyers. By the late nineteenth century, Chinese artists, like

CHESS SET, INDIA, IVORY, C. 1930

By the 20th century, Indian artisans began looking toward their own traditions as themes for chessmen. Sets began to appear based on the epics, legends, and stories of India. The Hindu epic, the Ramayana, became a favorite source of inspiration. The epic tells the story of Rama, his royal birth, youth, and eventual marriage to Sita. Shortly afterwards, Rama was displaced as rightful heir and banished from court. Rama retreats to a nearby forest where the demon king Ravana seizes Sita and carries her off. This set illustrates the ensuing battle between Ravana and Prince Rama for Sita. While Ravana, here shown with ten heads, leads an army composed of horrible creatures, Rama and his brother, Lakshamana, are aided by an army of monkeys who have magical powers. In the end, Prince Rama wins and eventually regains his throne.

143

their counterparts in India, had begun making fantastically embellished conventional sets based on European styles.

Over the course of the next century, as the world opened up to business, travelers, and, regrettably, war, artists living and working in the countless societies and cultures around the globe discovered that chess sets made for tourists sell. By the end of the twentieth century, chess sets had become part of the ubiquitous tourist trade found in airports and shops all over the world. Yet even as the twentieth century took hold, artists began to seriously—and sometimes not so seriously—explore new forms, shapes, and themes even as others tried to reinvent the game by invigorating it with new ideas and technologies. The range of subjects, materials, and styles found in chess sets from the twentieth century are not only surprising, but inspiring.

QUEEN, KNIGHT, BISHOP, AND TWO PAWNS, INUIT, WALRUS IVORY, 1962

Almost immediately after contact with Europeans in the 18th century, Inuit carvers began creating items for trade from whale bone and walrus ivory. These items included small sculptures, scrimshaw tusks, cribbage boards, and canes. By the 19th and early 20th century, they were making chess sets. Magnificent sets like this one, provide a glimpse into the world of the far north. The pawns in this set represent igloos. Contrary to popular belief, only Inuit of the central Arctic built snowhouses and then only used them for a temporary base during the winter seal-hunting season.

le Cavalier déraille ~ le Pion fait l'espion

CHAPTER SEVEN

THE TWENTIETH CENTURY AND BEYOND

BY THE BEGINNING of the twentieth century, chess had circumvented the globe. It was played in more nations and by more people throughout the world than perhaps in its first thousand years combined. Like the twentieth century itself, it came to represent a dizzying array of meanings. Diverse groups played the game for diverse reasons. Artists, like Marcel Duchamp, saw in chess pristine beauty and order. Soviet propagandists perceived the game as a chance to promote Soviet ideologies. And teachers used it to foster logical thinking skills. Most of all, chess became an indicator of greatness.

The first hurdle facing chess in the new century was, ironically, warfare. World War I was a catastrophe for Europe and other parts of the world. It left millions dead, missing, or horribly wounded. Beyond the immediacy of the conflict itself, it had a tremendous long-term impact on many different facets of life, from the distribution of food to cross-

CHESS SET AND BOARD, UNITED STATES, POLISHED BRONZE AND ENAMEL, 1962

For decades, beginning in 1926, Man Ray (1890–1976), one of the founders of the New York City Dada group, designed and made chess sets. He and other well-known artists at the time enjoyed playing chess. One of them, Dada artist Marcel Duchamp (1887–1968), was obsessed by the game. In the set shown here, Ray used geometric shapes with universal symbols to distinguish the pieces from one another.

147

CHESS SET, FRANCE, BACCARAT MOLDED GLASS, 20TH CENTURY

This set represents the political situation surrounding Czechoslovakia prior to and during World War II. The king is rendered as the Czech leader, Jan Masaryk (1886–1948), who in the 1940s was the foreign minister of the exiled Czechoslovakian government in London. For much of the 20th century politics would be mirrored in chess set designs just as the game itself would become another psychological skirmish in the political posturing of the Cold War. The Baccarat Glass Company was established in 1765, and is most renowned for its paperweights and tableware.

ing borders. The so-called war to end all wars left a legacy that was to hang like a dark cloud over much of Europe over the next two decades. In the aftermath of the conflict, individual chess organizations found it much more difficult to maintain competitive and international play.

While the recovery of chess was slow in Europe, elsewhere it was a different matter. In North America, Australia, and India—where the Western game had been introduced—chess continued to gain ground. But with the growing numbers of people from countries around the world interested in playing, the lack of international standards made it increasingly more difficult to organize international matches and tournaments.

In 1924 the Federation Internationale des Échecs (FIDE), the

World Chess Federation, was founded to oversee increasingly complex international competitive play. Competition rules and levels of play were introduced streamlining and organizing international competitions. Eventually, all competitive players were ranked according to levels. Perhaps one of the most significant outcomes of its mission was the development of a junior level for young players, thus ensuring the continuation of the game into the twenty-first century.

As a result, the game became extraordinarily competitive. Prizes became larger, and substantially more attractive. Large purses provided incentives that lured larger numbers of skilled players. As the frequency of tournaments increased, for the first time players also found that they could make a substantial living at chess. The largest of these prizes also whetted the attention of the general public, and as a consequence, considerable notice and support was given to the game. Gainful employment of chess masters along with public support provided a stabilizing influence on the game.

By mid-century, tournament play heated up as nations began to recognize both the social and political cachet of the game. At times it almost seemed as if the fate of nations hung in the balance. As the Cold War accelerated, chess became a flash point for the increasingly complex propaganda games played by the key international powers—namely the United States and the Soviet Union.

The Soviet Union identified with this strategy most strongly. Eager to impress upon the West the ideological premise of communism, the Soviet Union expended a tremendous effort in the development of its chess program. Talented players were from a young age sought, trained, supported, and sponsored. In return they were expected to win, and with the advantages of their training, they often did. As a consequence, the Soviet Union dominated international play for the

CHESS SET AND BOARD, FRANCE, LALIQUE MOLDED GLASS, 20TH CENTURY

In the 20th century a number of European glass-making firms, including Lalique, tried their hand at making chess sets. René Lalique (1860–1945) pioneered a frosted glass technique, preferring the more subtle look of white on white to the riot of colors that his contemporaries Daum and Gallé favored. He also produced less expensive, molded pieces, allowing him to sell to a broader market.

better part of the twentieth century. That is, until American champion Bobby Fischer burst onto the scene in the 1960s, momentarily diverting it to American dominance. The energy and money that the Soviets put into the development of players of international merit was perhaps the most significant influence on the game of chess in the last half of the twentieth century.

Throughout the twentieth century, however, the game was more than an opportunity for political gesturing and propaganda. Increasingly larger prizes, the excitement of international competition, and many of the personalities involved, such as Fischer, Anatoly Karpov, and Garry Kasparov all served to increase and further broaden the popularity of the game. Consequently, chess was transformed from celebrity status into a grassroots movement in small communities around the world. Suddenly, local neighborhoods and schools developed chess clubs, encouraging competition among amateur players from all backgrounds. Local clubs quickly banded into regional groups

Facing page, bottom:

CHESS SET, GERMAN, VILLEROY & BOCH, COBALT AND CLEAR GLASS, C. 1975-1992

Like Lalique and Baccarat, the firm of Villeroy & Boch also tried their hand at designing a chess set. Unlike the others, this one is designed in a conventional style. However, its real beauty lies in the jewel-like glow of refracted light thrown by the pieces on their mirrored board. Villeroy & Boch, established in 1748, is famous for their fine tableware.

Facing page, top:

CHESS SET, UNITED STATES, MOLDED CERAMIC, C. 1960

Lewis Carroll's novels, and the subsequent Disney movie, *Alice in Wonderland*, have inspired the design of several chess sets. Interestingly, the original book illustrations for the Queen and her court by artist Sir John Tenniel for *Through the Looking Glass–And What Alice Found There*, were inspired by 19th-century Barleycorn sets. This set was designed by Harm Robinson.

Facing page, middle:

CHESS SET, UNITED STATES, NUTS AND BOLTS DESIGN, HARDWARE, LATE 20TH CENTURY

The idea of using nuts and bolts to create chess sets probably grew out of the experiments made by Dada artists. The essence of the Dada art movement was to juxtapose unrelated everyday objects and situations to create unexpected images from completely familiar sources. Here the craftsman has echoed the design of traditional chessmen by carefully selecting familiar hardware pieces.

153

PLAYING SET, CAMBODIA, IVORY, EARLY 20TH CENTURY

Cambodian sets, like this one, were not made for trade with the West. They were meant for play by Cambodians. The only familiar piece to Western eyes is the knight, represented by a horse. The others seem to be abstract designs based on sea shells. In fact, Cambodian playing sets typically use real shells as pawns, called fishes by the players. Similar sets are used in neighboring Thailand, and it is likely that this game, slightly modified, was inherited from India several centuries ago.

Right:

CHESS SET, MEXICO, TARASCAN INDIANS, MADRONA AND JABONCILLO WOODS, AND BONE, C. 1944

In the first half of the 20th century, the Tarascan Indians of Mexico made these fine chess sets on a lathe and embellished the pieces with small bits of carved bone. Although the Tarascan Indians may have originally learned the lathe technique from the Spaniards, the design is reminiscent of the Régence style, popular in France in the 19th century. It is interesting to note that in the 1860s France became involved in Mexican politics, persuading Mexico to create a monarchy and crown the archduke of Austria as Emperor Maximilian (1832–1867). The influence of French design on the sets made by the Tarascan Indians in the 20th century may be a reflection of French influence during the turbulent decades of the previous century.

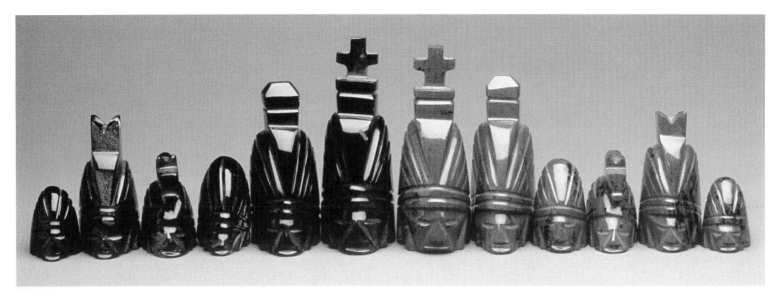

Above:

CHESS SET, MEXICO, STONE
C. 1968

Mexican artisans have been master stone carvers for hundreds of years and the material is frequently used today to create chess sets for the tourist market. Although alabaster is more widely used, many fine sets have been crafted in obsidian. Chess sets, like this one, may be inspired by the carvings found on monuments or by prints made from surviving texts, such as the *Codex Zouche-Nuttall* of the Mixtec people (1521). The symbols on top of each figure were borrowed from European designs to help identify the pieces.

to hold tournaments. Now anyone who wanted to could enjoy tournament play. Mass-produced chess sets, inexpensive and widely available, made it even easier for people at all economic levels to play the game.

Perhaps because of its intellectual association, as chess became more democratic during the course of the twentieth century, it quickly became linked with the act of learning itself. Educators, who had been encouraging chess clubs as a way to develop confidence, have more recently been using the game as a teaching aid in the classroom. Schools now not only offer chess as an extracurricular activity but use it to develop critical thinking skills, logical deduction, and the concept of consequences among students as young as kindergarten age.

Truely, wherever chess is played, it is here to stay. More than any other period in history, the game can be found in almost every corner of the globe. Its presence is so pervasive that when casting about for a recognizable human activity that would believably be played centuries from now, the writers of the American television show, *Star Trek*, selected chess as the obvious choice.

PLAYING PIECES IN THE 20TH CENTURY

The types and styles of chessmen made throughout the century mushroomed exponentially, reflecting the growing interest and popularity of the game by players and collectors alike. And while artists and craftspeople around the world continued to make one-of-a-kind sets of superior quality and sophistication, increased demand and modern manufacturing techniques led to a wide diversity of styles and themes that could now be mass-produced and sold at a range of prices.

This was made possible by the invention and development of resins and plastics. Durable and inexpensive, plastic can rival or even imitate rare and costly materials such as ivory. It can be molded, carved,

CHESS SET AND BOARD, UNITED STATES, EXUDED ALUMINUM, 1983

Chess sets in the 20th century were designed and made for a variety of purposes beyond playing. Some comment on society or politics. Others, with their ostentatious display, reflect great wealth and status. Still others are meant to be presentation pieces, reflecting on the generosity and character of the giver. This set was designed by Scott Wolfe for Columbia Aluminum. It is one of 150 sets made to be distributed to business partners and associates as a corporate gift.

157

CHESS SET, NIGERIA, THORNWOOD, C. 1930–1960S

As Africa began to attract tourism, local artists and carvers began to manufacture items for the trade, including chess sets. Popular sets were those depicting regional people and wildlife. Although Nigerian sets sometimes depict the Yoruba in opposition to the Hausa people of Nigeria, both sides of this set seemed to represent the Yoruba people. It is made of thornwood, a relatively lightweight wood of the region favored by the carvers.

CHESS SET, MALAWI, IVORY AND EBONY, 1960

Tourists to Africa affected the design of chess sets in a variety of different ways. The buyer of this set provided Jackson, a carver belonging to the Nyanda tribe, with drawings of African animals.

158

KING AND CHESS SET, MOZAMBIQUE, MAKONDE, EBONY AND YELLOWWOOD, C. 1950

The Makonde are an East African tribal group with a strong carving tradition. Most live in Mozambique but the tribe extends across the border into southern Tanzania. Makonde artists have developed a chess set design featuring portraits of their people representing the king, queen, bishop, and pawns. Round thatched huts and giraffes provide the inspiration for the rooks and knights. In finer sets like this one, each of the carved portraits present distinctly different individuals, perhaps people the artist knew. Although Makonde artists prefer to carve with white hardwood and an African blackwood, called *mphingo*, they also use yellowwood and ebony.

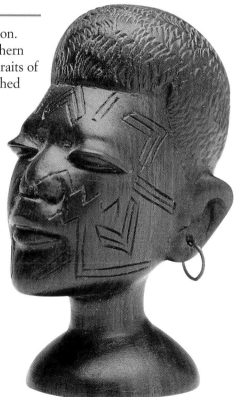

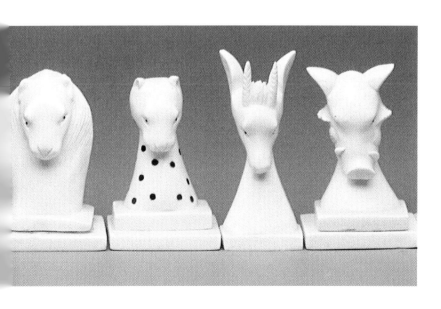

or turned on a lathe, and gives manufacturers the ability to produce exacting replicas of earlier historical chess pieces. In recent years, a number of late medieval representational sets, including the Lewis Chessmen, have been cast as reproductions for sale at relatively afford-able prices.

At the same time, traditionally manufactured chess sets prolifer-ated. Popular styles loosely based on older playing sets, such as the English Staunton or the French Régence styles of the preceding cen-tury, were produced by the thousands.

The desire for novelty has also influenced makers to alter the game itself—this time not in its rules, but rather in its dimensions. The multilevel chessboard used on the television show *Star Trek*, originally conceived as a futuristic look at chess, caught on in the popular imag-ination, and ultimately it was widely marketed. More recently, a ver-sion designed and produced in the United States offered an unusual approach by providing a circular, movable board on which the pieces are laid out. The game is played with the same rules, but the board revolves in a circular pattern around a central focal point.

Individual chess set designs also appeared as hobbyists took up the challenge. Even though interpretations on the Régence and Staunton styles were initially popular, skilled hobbyists also began trying their hand at representational designs. As the century progressed, they began to experiment, producing an astonishing array of sets repre-senting a wide range of themes, including sets made from recycled computer components.

CHESS SET AND BOARD, FRANCE, PAINTED LEAD, LATE 20TH CENTURY

As the 20th century progressed and natural habitats were threatened or disappeared, more and more people became interested in, and aware of, natural ecosystems found throughout the globe. This set presents the animals found living in and around the Sea of Barentz in the Arctic Circle on a board incorporating a hydrographic map of the region. Here, the artist, Mrs. D'Olliamson, has created a miniature model of the ecosystem of the Sea of Barentz.

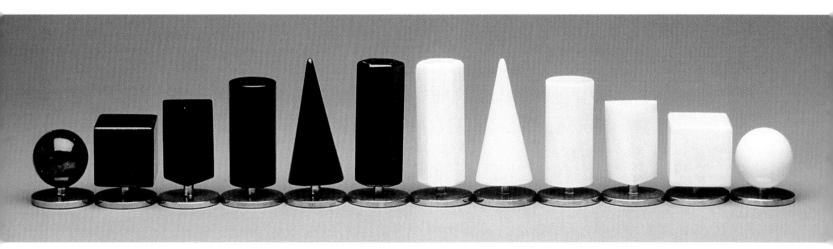

CHESS SET, ITALY, STONE, 1957

Italy has been extremely receptive to the modern art movements of the 20th century, which most certainly influenced the design of this set, created by the firm G. Bessi in Volterra, Italy.

INSPIRED BY ART

As the twentieth century witnessed a continued increase in the availability of chess sets, it also witnessed an intellectual reaction to mass production and traditional forms and subjects. Dissatisfied with the older styles and themes, which seemed trite and out of date, a number of artists began to experiment with chess set design. Like the modern art movements of the first three or four decades of the century that they came from, artist-designed sets were meant to break the mold yet also provide a unique and satisfying experience for the player.

One of the first significant attempts to redefine the chess piece in the early part of the century was made by the German designer Josef Hartwig in 1924. A master craftsman at the famous Bauhaus School

162

CHESS SET, UNITED STATES, CERAMIC, C. 1960

This set comprises an odd assortment of characters whose exaggerated features and postures could suggest a variety of stories from the turmoil of Richard Daley's tenure in Chicago in the 1960s to one of the more popular Shakespearean plays of the century, *A Midsummer Night's Dream*. All that can be said is that the pieces exhibit a biting sarcasm that would be appropriate to either story. Consequently, the set highlights a growing issue between collectors and historians of the game. When sets are collected out of context and the associated history is lost, it can be anyone's guess as to what the set really represents.

CHESS SET, FRENCH, WOOD, 1944

In the 1940s, a number of artists living in New York City began experimenting with chess set designs. The project became so widespread that an exhibition was suggested and planned. This set was exhibited by Max Ernst (1891–1976) in *The Imagery of Chess* show in 1944 at the Julien Levy Gallery in New York. It was originally conceived on a trip to the beach with the gallery's owner, Julien Levy. As a player and artist, Ernst remained sensitive to the need for well-balanced and easily recognizable pieces. Each piece is a brilliant abstracted interpretation of traditional playing pieces. Over time, several versions of it have been produced in a variety of materials.

near Dessau, Germany, prior to World War II, Hartwig created a chess set design based on the function of the pieces, not on their names or what they might represent. Although his elegant geometrical style, symbolizing the movement of individual pieces, failed to capture the popular imagination, they are still sold today.

Yet for the better part of the century artists continued to experiment with the shape and form of chess pieces. This is hardly surprising. At a time in which artists were constantly challenging viewpoints by presenting or altering traditional concepts, images, and things into new contexts and settings, they could not have found better objects to manipulate than chess pieces. Chess was everyman's game—familiar to young and old alike. Those artists most interested in the manipulation of the everyday—the Dadaists and Surrealists—seemed especially drawn toward redesigning chess pieces. As well-known objects, the essential six playing pieces offered them both an opportunity to reshape the image of chess and, at the same time, they presented interesting solutions to the problems posed by the pieces.

One of the more significant events in chess design of the twentieth century was an exhibition held at the Julien Levy Gallery in New York City in 1944. *The Imagery of Chess* brought such artists as Alexander Calder, Max Ernst, Man Ray, Isamu Noguchi, Yves Tanguy, and others together to create unique chess sets for the modern era. Undoubtedly, the exhibition gave impetus to a whole new way of looking at chess sets and, since then, artists continue to experiment with a wide range of themes and materials.

THE COLLECTING PHENOMENA

Rich-looking sets might be made for the mass-market, but they are also made for the ever-growing collectors' market. By mid-century, collectors drawn by shared interests began banding together into semiformal groups. In 1984, this pattern culminated in the establishment of Chess Collectors International, and subsequent national and regional affiliations. Such groups, not only infused new energy into the antiques trade but opened new markets by encouraging artists and manufacturers to produce inventive and unusual sets for sale. Likewise, their interests have fueled scholarly research and

study of the history of chess and its playing pieces in the closing decades of the twentieth century.

Generally less interested in the advancement of play, collectors covet a variety of styles from the antique to the novel. Sets might be purchased from street vendors in tourist destinations or from makers who design exclusively for the collector. Besides individual artists and craftspeople creating one-of-a-kind examples, a number of manufacturers specialize in quality chess sets. Among them are Anri and Vasari of Italy and the Franklin Mint and The House of Staunton in the United States.

THE FUTURE

The computer, arguably the most significant invention of the twentieth century, may be the future of chess. Chess games for the computer have taken the play and the pieces beyond the physical limitations of the real world. Even more significantly, Internet access provides the means for players living thousands of miles apart to engage in a game.

Ideas about machines playing chess have circulated since the introduction of the Automaton Chess Player by Wolfgang von Kempelen in the eighteenth century. With a person concealed inside of the device it gave the impression that a machine could play chess. Today, computers run sophisticated programs that not only teach the game but provide challenges for players at all skill levels. Perhaps

CHESS SET AND BOARD, ITALY, GILDED AND SILVERED BRONZE, AND MARBLE, 20TH CENTURY

Italy has been the home of a number of manufacturers who have created extraordinarily rich and ornate sets for the luxury and collectors' market. Among them are the firms of Italfama and Vasari. These companies look to the past for their inspiration, presenting historical events or noted personalities. This one represents the court of Louis XIII.

the most significant chess event of the century took place in 1997 when Garry Kasparov, world chess champion, lost a match to Deep Blue, the IBM computer programmed with countless grand master moves and strategies.

As for the game itself, it continues to evolve. It is a work in progress and just when it seems that little more can be imagined, some new interpretation comes along and the game alters. Sometimes the changes are slight and gradual. Sometimes they are fast and dramatic. But will new advances in computer technology make conventional chess sets obsolete? Hopefully not. For as long as there are players and collectors who take as much pleasure in the beauty of the chessmen as they do in the play of the game, chess will continue much the way it has for centuries. The past has shown us that much about the future.

CHESS SET AND BOARD, GREECE, BRONZE, 20TH CENTURY

The past has always been a rich treasure house of ideas for chess sets. Over the course of the 20th century, archaeologists of the ancient Mediterranean world have brought to light the sculptural forms of the Archaic Greek people. This set is based on the Aegean art of the early Bronze Age found on the Cycladic Islands of the southeastern coast of Greece. The board is made from marble.

BIBLIOGRAPHY

The following is a selection of sources that I found the most useful; each, in its own way, will lead the attentive reader deeper into the history of chess and chess sets.

The Chess Collector. The Journal of Chess Collectors International.
The pages of this journal are inspiring, fascinating, and interesting; perhaps more importantly, they provide up-to-date information on the development of chess and chess pieces.

Dennis, Jessie McNab, and Wilkinson, Charles K., *Chess: East and West, Past and Present.*
New York: The Metropolitan Museum of Art, 1968. This book has a summary of the history of chess, and it portrays the richness of the chess set collection housed at the Metropolitan Museum of Art.

Eales, Richard. *Chess: The History of a Game.* New York: Facts on File Publications, 1985.
This excellent, well-written book is a must-read for anyone interested in the history of the game.

Graham, F. Lanier. *Chess Sets.* New York: Walker and Company, 1968.
Lanier's critical approach toward the development of the form and the shape of chess pieces, as well as its art-historical format, makes this slim volume worth reading.

Keats, Victor. *The Illustrated Guide to World Chess Sets.* New York: St. Martin's Press, 1985.
This guide is an exhaustive listing of chess sets created around the world over the course of several centuries, and thus an excellent resource.

Liddell, Donald M. *Chessmen.* London: George G. Harrap & Co. Ltd., 1938.
Although the text is quaint, the thorough listing in the appendix of antique chess sets and their locations makes it an invaluable reference.

Linder, I. M. *The Art of Chess Pieces.* Moscow: H.G.S. Publishers, 1994.
The focus of this beautifully illustrated volume is on chess and chess pieces from the Russian point of view, and it significantly presents little-known examples of eastern European and Russian sets from antiquity onward.

Murray, H.J.R. *A History of Chess.* Oxford: Oxford University Press, 1913.
Although at times ponderous, this book is extremely valuable not only as a definitive text on the history of chess, but also because Murray quotes in great detail the numerous references about chess from older literary texts, rather than simply referring to them.

Wichmann, Hans and Siegfried. *Chess: The Story of Chesspieces from Antiquity to Modern Times.*
New York: Crown Publishers, 1960. The black-and-white photographs in this volume stunningly present a visual record of chess sets from the earliest time, and the supporting catalogue information is invaluable.

Williams, Gareth. *Master Pieces: The Architecture of Chess.* New York: Viking Studio, 2000. This illustrated small-format book is chock-full of interesting stories and information about the game and its playing pieces.

PICTURE CREDITS

All photos © Maryhill Museum of Art, Goldendale, Washington, except as listed below

INDEX
Page numbers in **boldface** refer to illustrations.

ACKNOWLEDGMENTS

I would like to gratefully acknowledge everyone who has ever studied and written about the history of chess and the game's playing pieces. Their collective studies have been a tremendous asset to me. I could not have done it without them. I would particularly like to recognize H.J.R. Murray. Insufficient credit is given to this man whose passion and love of the game resulted in a work of extraordinary scholarship, *A History of Chess,* and to whom all of us who write about chess owe a great debt. I would also like to acknowledge all the members, collectors, and scholars of Chess Collectors International. Their enthusiasm and hard work have been a tremendous boost to the scholarship of the game. On a personal level, I would like to especially thank two of their members: Mrs. Kay Jahn Morry and Mr. Erwin Ezzes. They not only introduced me to this wonderful and exciting world, but have been exceptionally kind and supportive over the years. Finally, but not least, I would like to thank Richard J. Berenson, who suggested this book and somehow got me to finish it.